The Thing Contained

THEORY OF THE TRAGIC

BLOOMINGTON / LONDON

The Thing Contained

Theory of the Tragic

Laurence Michel

Indiana University Press

As palomides hunted the questing beast, [Miss Groby] hunted
the Figure of Speech. She hunted it through the clangorous
halls of Shakespeare and through the green forests of Scott. . . .
At first I began to fear that all the characters in Shakespeare
and Scott were crazy. They confused cause with effect, the
sign for the thing signified, the thing held for the thing
holding it. But after a while I began to suspect that it was
I myself who was crazy. I would find myself lying awake at
night saying over and over, "The thinger for the thing contained."
In a great but probably misguided attempt to keep my mind on
its hinges, I would stare at the ceiling and try to think of
an example of the Thing Contained for the Container. . . .
I dream of my old English teacher occasionally. It seems that
we are always in Sherwood Forest and that from far away I can
hear Robin Hood winding his silver horn.

"Drat that man for making such a racket on his cornet!"
cries Miss Groby. "He scared away a perfectly darling Container
for the Thing Contained, a great, big, beautiful one. It leaped
right back into its context when that man blew that cornet.
It was the most wonderful Container for the Thing Contained I
ever saw here in the Forest of Arden."

"This is Sherwood Forest," I say to her.

"That doesn't make any difference at all that I can see,"
she says to me.

Then I wake up, tossing and moaning.

James Thurber, *My World and Welcome to It*

The artist usually sets out—or used to—to point a moral
and adorn a tale. The tale, however, points the other way,
as a rule. Two blankly opposing morals, the artist's and the
tale's. Never trust the artist. Trust the tale. The proper
function of a critic is to save the tale from the artist who created it.

D. H. Lawrence, *Studies in Classic American Literature*

Contents

Preface

THIS BOOK BEGAN WHEN THE ENGLISH DEPARTMENT OF Wayne State University invited me to give a series of lectures in the fall of 1965. I was glad of the opportunity to pull together certain ideas about tragedy which had been accumulating in my head and my files and my nerve-endings; the result, however, was put-together, juxtaposed, rather than systematic or methodical. This was worrisome for a while, but I have persuaded myself (and a publisher, to whom I am grateful for faith and support) that such a paratactic and adumbratory presentation is a virtue, not a defect: especially in dealing with tragedy, which has long suffered from attempts to reduce it to a well-made, wrapped-up rationale. Corroboration of the validity of such elusiveness came from Francis Bacon, through the good offices of Marshall McLuhan and Norman O. Brown:

> Truth, a broken body; fragments, or aphorisms; as opposed to systematic form or methods; "Aphorisms, representing a knowledge broken, do invite men to inquire farther; whereas Methods, carrying the show of a total, do secure men, as if they were at furthest."

Meaning is not in things but in between; in the iridescence, the inter-
play; in the interconnections; at the intersections, at the crossroads.

Instead of the deadwood of systems, the tree of life; ramifications;
branched thoughts new-grown with pleasant pain. (*Love's Body*)[1]

I hope that the pains of reading these branched suggestions may be
as pleasant as those taken in their ramification. Also, I have been
emboldened to venture into amateur author-psychology by testimony from artists themselves: Wallace Stevens reports and demonstrates that "the acquisitions of poetry are fortuitous; *trouvailles*";
the mind "begets in resemblance and gives birth to an unexpected
possession of the object."[2] The *I* of John Barth's *Floating Opera*
recognizes and acknowledges his *It:*

> this observation ["do you *really* want to kill yourself?"] died in the
> womb, itself asphyxiated by the demon "why not"—that over-
> whelming genie I'd released from his bottle earlier in the evening,
> having struggled unknowingly with the cork for most of my life,
> and who now filled my mind as completely and lethally as the gas
> that was filling the room. There was no escaping this genie. . . .[3]

As an outside examiner for an honors seminar in tragedy, I once
tried the following congeries-conundrum as the rubric for an essay
examination:

> TRAGEDY can be seen, from one set of presuppositions, as a sym-
>
> metrical Poseidonian trident: ⅃⏐⌐ Something we all call the
> tragic vision is the handle; we can apprehend it, grab hold of it,
> somewhere along its length, however awkwardly or loosely or at
> the wrong end or off the balance point. The right-hand prong points
> at the epic, humanistic, heroic, affirmative; the life-forces; greatness
> of the human spirit; the dream of innocence; tragic optimism. Its
> barb hooks into psychological and ethical tangles which, when
> brought to the surface, can be understood, if not resolved. The
> left-hand prong points at the realm of the in-, super-, anti-, or
> a-human; indifferent or capricious or hostile power; chaos, vanity,
> nihilism; the death-forces; the fact of guilt; tragic pessimism. Its

barb catches gobbets of piety, qualm, demonism. The central prong is longer, double-barbed, in line with the main thrust of the handle. It harpoons the heart of Reality and, having drawn in the dilemma-horns to the juxtaposed compass of aesthetic paradox, plucks out the mystery, balanced on the twin shoulders of I-thou, yea-and-nay, life-in-death, not only/but also.

Another version of the trident is asymmetrical: The handle is still in the middle, but the longest prong is the left-handed one, and two of the barbs hook to the left. Tragedy harpoons reality, but its bias is sinister. In order to get heroic humanism in far enough to hook onto any appreciable amount of usable power, the trident has to plunge the death-probes deeper than is safe, and penetrate the nucleus long enough for it to go critical. The chain reaction becomes self-sustaining; coming up, the strong pull to the left weakens the hold of right still further; the demon of anarchy, now autonomous, poisons the would-be moderator, and emerges into the phenomenal world a bomb of evil—uncontrollable power and deadly radiation. It destroys itself and all around it, leaving only a few fission fragments, themselves contaminated. There is the peace of death, nearly all poison spent; equilibrium is achieved, the catharsis of entropy.

There is of course a right-handed trident: which some fishermen use for dexterously scratching the back of the Reality-Leviathan; on closer inspection it turns out to have a very short handle, slanted and off-center. Used as it must be, this glorified clam-rake searches no vitals, but pulls out pre-planted plums, saying "What a good boy am I." The would-be subversive left barb trails along on its back, feebly turning up a small *felix culpa* or two to be added to the chowder for seasoning.

The question to be answered was, Which of these is the true, the right, tragic instrument? To my perhaps unwarranted disappointment, all nine of the bright and able candidates for honors chose the first. The following essays are an attempt to argue for the primacy and legitimacy of the bar sinister.

Acknowledgements

Grateful acknowledgements are due, and are hereby proffered, to ALBERT COOK, LIONEL ABEL, NORMAN RABKIN, and ARTHUR EFRON for critical reading and suggestions; to RICHARD SEWALL and MAX BLUESTONE for past inspiration and encouragement; and to JOHN I. SEWALL for making available to me his own "Liberty Hall" in Maine, where a large part of the writing was done.

L. M.

Buffalo, N.Y., 1970

The Thing Contained

THEORY OF THE TRAGIC

I

Aspects of Tragedy: Form and Feature

I

THE MAJOR THESIS OF THIS BOOK IS THAT THE ESSENCE of tragedy—that which makes it what it is and not something else —is demonic, ir- or anti-rational, Dionysian. If we try to substitute the Apollonian overlay for the thing itself, we are likely to go wrong, misapprehend it, and consequently attenuate and falsify its value. Nietzsche understood this: "At the point that matters most the Apollonian illusion has been broken through and destroyed." T. S. Eliot, in endorsing G. Wilson Knight's search for the underlying pattern in Shakespeare, concluded that "poetry is poetry, and the surface is as marvellous as the core"—but he did not (on that occasion at least) intimate the further phenomenon that in tragic poetry the core exhibits itself on the surface, and usurps it. W. H. Auden's two lyres alternate and complement one another, "related by antithesis"—but compromise between them is bad for both; the words of Mercury are harsh after the songs of Apollo. "You that way—we this way."[1] In tragedy, at least, the hermetic seems to be primordial, and it is the *Ding an sich:* the Thinger, the Content, the Thing Contained. Critics, teachers, philosophers, ethicians have largely refused to grant this primacy, and have erected structures of tragedy like Spenserian Houses of Pride: squared brick veneered with golden foil, goodly heaps to behold, crowned with timely dials and led up to by broad and beaten highways; but only facades mounted on sand, whose hinder parts are cunningly painted ruins.[2] Even the artists themselves, in their prosaic or abstractive moments, more often than not have tried to cabin and confine their own familiar demons.

The epic (epideictic?) poets have delivered themselves, more or less explicitly and at length, on what they were programmatically intending to do, but more often than not the poem is at variance with the program. "Fierce warres and faithfull loves shall moralize my song," Spenser announces in the Proem to the opening Book of Holiness;[3] but once having evoked demonic Despair, he gives him a persuasive voice to the contrary:

> The lenger life, I wote, the greater sin,
> The greater sin, the greater punishment:
> All those great battels, which thou boasts to win,
> Through strife and blood-shed, and avengement,
> Now praysed, hereafter deare thou shalt repent:
> For life must life, and blood must blood repay.[4]

It takes Una's fierce assertion of the Calvinist doctrine of election to foil this diabolic moralist; and that his force is only scotched, not killed, is proved in the poetic way, by tacit parallel, when Contemplation himself, to whom Una has brought the knight for confirmation in his virtue, even in the midst of his exhortation to worthy service, deeds of arms, and famous victory, voices the same dilemma:

> Thenceforth the suitt of earthly conquest shonne,
> And wash thy hands from guilt of bloudy field;
> For blood can nought but sin, and wars but sorrow yield.[5]

The same thing happens when the elaborate casuistry underlying the justification of achieving Temperance through controlled irascibility is undercut not only by Phaedria's appealing quietism, but, in parallel circumstances, by Medina's crying shame upon the knightly ferocity of both Guyon and Sans Loy. Spenser's virtuous and gently disciplined gentlemen behave like wild boars and mad dogs when they are supposed to be pointing the moral; Arthur himself is not proof against the subversive adjectives which come swarming up from Spenser's undermind to adorn the tale. Even in a tournament, the commencement exercises of chivalric pedagogy, Arthegall "tyrannizes" behind his shield (on which is written "*Salvagesse sans finesse*, shewing secret wit"), hewing and slashing like a lion in his bloody game so that "every one gan shun his dreadful sight, No lesse then death itselfe, in daungerous affright."[6] This lamentable Knight of Justice also finds himself rescued from the monstrous regiment of women by a *good* virago, Britomart, who is yet, in the poetry, indistinguishable from Radegund in either fierce warlikeness or man-devouring, viscerally faithful "love" of Arthegall. The spectre of Queen Elizabeth-Mercilla-dread-sovereign-female shedding crocodile tears (in her incarnation as the Isis-dream Britomart, she has already sexually ingested the crocodile) while her tame male character assassins Zeal-Walsingham and Kingdoms Care-Burleigh set Queen Mary up for extermination, haunts not only Book V but Books III–IV too. Spenser was going to produce, by "a pleasing analysis of all," a paradigm of glory and magnificence in his "general intention." "But," being a poet he realizes on second thought, "by occasion hereof many other adventures are intermeddled, but rather as accidents than intendments: as the love of Britomart, the overthrow of Marinell, the misery of Florimell, the vertousness of Belphoebe, the laciviousness of Hellenora, and many the like."[7] For purposes of moralizing, a curiously incongrous set of *like* things. Accident betrays intendment; the thing contained overflows and envelops the container.

Milton, adventurously pursuing things unattempted before (that is, bringing death and all woe into the world; evoking the demon), proposes to argue, assert, and justify God's ways to men. Whether he succeeded in the disposing (the poetry) in either glorifying God or making the devil an ass has long been a troublesome moot question. Wordsworth, yearning to overgo Milton and write "some philosophic Song of Truth that cherishes our daily life,"[8] that would penetrate to the real universal heavenly region (the Mind of Man, not a Miltonic sultanate inhabited by choirs of shouting angels), found as soon as he got into his prelude that the god of *his* idolatry was really his own individual, daemonic self. He tried off and on for thirty-five years to put some parts of this pantheistic genie back into Christian bottles, but the 1850 text of *The Prelude* is commonly cited as witness to the inevitable failure of such an attempt.[9]

Shakespeare was mostly a dramatic poet, and we find him addressing himself directly to his process and technique very occasionally. Early, there is the long excursus in *Lucrece* on synecdoche and the painter's ability to imitate reality and on the advantages and dangers of collaborating with the artist:

> For much imaginary work was there.
> Conceit deceitful, so compact, so kind,
> That for Achilles' image stood his spear
> Gripped in an armed hand: himself behind
> Was left unseen save to the eye of mind.
>   A hand, a foot, a face, a leg, a head,
>   Stood for the whole to be imagined.

> And from the walls of strong besieged Troy
> When their brave hope, bold Hector, marched to field,
> Stood many Trojan mothers sharing joy
> To see their youthful sons bright weapons wield.
> And to the hope they such odd action yield
>   That through their light joy seemed to appear,
>   Like bright things stained, a kind of heavy fear.[10]

Lucrece seeks "for means to mourn some newer way," and drawn by the "sweet observance" of the painter of Troy's woes, "set awork" by his "conceit deceitful," "sad tales doth tell To pencil'd pensiveness and colour'd sorrow: She lends them words, and she their looks doth borrow." As soon as she tries to lend words, however, she finds them slippery and subject to manipulation by the imagination, so that they say the opposite of what she intends:

> "It cannot be," quoth she, "that so much guile"—
> She would have said "can lurk in such a look";
> But Tarquin's shape came in her mind the while
> And from her tongue "can lurk" from "cannot" took:
> "It cannot be" she in that sense forsook
>   And turn'd it thus: "It cannot be, I find
>   But such a face should bear a wicked mind;
>
> For even as subtill Sinon here is painted,
> So sober-sad, so weary, and so mild,
> As if with grief or travail he had fainted,
> To me came Tarquin armed, so beguil'd
> With outward honesty, but yet defil'd
>   With inward vice . . . ."[11]

She does achieve some relief from this activity, but it is at the expense of her former faith in the reality of appearances: she "chid the painter for his wondrous skill" in making the treacherous Sinon into "so fair a form" and recognizes that "these contraries such unity do hold, Only to flatter fools and make them bold." Partial catharsis comes, after the ebb and flow of passion, she "Being from the feeling of her own grief brought By deep surmise of others detriment, Losing her woes in shows of discontent." Partial: "It easeth some, though none it ever cured." Spenser too allows himself an occasional outburst of piety to his daemon, usually when he catches himself at luxuriating in a celebration of pure, unmoralizable aestheticism or even hedonism: "O wondrous skill and sweet wit of the man," he exclaims of the tapestry-maker for the House of Busyrane, who, using gold thread

Like a discoloured snake, whose hidden snares
Through the greene gras his long bright burnished back declares,

portrayed all of Cupid's wars against the gods, including Leda and the Swan. This whole passage (III.xi.27–55), Britomart's ordeal by sight-temptation, is laced with the like remarks. And the whole episode, with Britomart emboldened to glut her "greedy eyes," to wonder and marvel at "the goodly ordinaunce of this rich place," even as she realizes in fascination that it was "false love" which was there displayed in "A thousand monstrous formes," and then to be admonished with the riddling "Be bolde, be bolde, . . . Be not too bold"—all this, supported by such identities of phrasing as "wondrous skill" and "sweet wit," "sweet observance," gives grounds for the not unlikely speculation that when Shakespeare mused upon the ambivalent power of imagination in a moral tale he found Spenser there before him, and took his cue from this high priest of the New Poetry, this eclectic and bold tale-adorning moral-pointer. The immediately preceding *Venus and Adonis* has been rescued for some years now from the limbo of "pretty sensuality" and recognized to be at least as full as *Hero and Leander* of burlesque and blasphemy against the goddess of sweaty passion.

Later in Shakespeare we encounter the curiously obtrusive, almost importunate use of the chorus in *Henry V*. Milton was to summon Urania down from heaven to help him do justice to his great theme; Shakespeare calls "O, for a muse of fire, that would ascend The brightest heaven of invention." So far, orthodox enough: he wants a mimesis adequate to his conception (or, to use the terms of that cool reasoner Theseus, a comprehensive container for his apprehensions).[12] But as he gets into what is involved (as we shall see in Chapter 2), the subsequent choruses betray the consequences of this high-minded enterprise. If the History Plays are epical—and it has been claimed that Shakespeare shared the providential view of the Tudor-myth chroniclers—not only the texture of the dramatic poetry therein but the very how-to-read-this-play program notes in the *Henry V* choruses are outspoken witnesses to the inability of the containing frame to hold the tragic Thing.

The Phoenix and the Turtle, while long recognized as enigmatic and metaphysical, is just now emerging into the cooler air of Chaucerian bird-play, where it doubtless belongs. As for the Sonnets, Murray Krieger (in *A Window to Criticism*) has enlisted them in his forces of poetic demonism; and though Shakespeare, the Willful poet, in Sonnet 74 claims his good spirit, his "better part," as the valuable and immortal thing held by the base body—"The worth of that is that which it contains"[13]—his word-corrupter has produced in the (linked) No. 73 a perfect specimen of autonomous counter-statement through tragic-plot syntax (see p. oo):

> In me thou see'st the glowing of such fire,
> That on the ashes of his youth doth lie
> As the deathbed whereon it must expire,
> Consumed with that which it was nourished by.

The difficulty with trying to obey Lawrence's quite sound admonition lies in discovering, in any given set of words, which is speaking and in control: the tale or the author.

II

When I began teaching what was then called a vertical course, about fifteen years ago, I was an ostensible, or at least ostentatious, empiric about tragedy. Read the stuff, I said, never mind the critics; absorb the tragedies, don't get bogged down in theory. But it could not work, of course, and the students and I soon found ourselves, even as we rather haughtily eschewed a definition, devising and using provisional formulas. We never called them that, since no one wanted to be tarred with the brush of formalism or accused of being a conformist. Yet, if a work of art has (or is) a beauteous form, surely we can come closest to grasping it (and perhaps become somewhat more beauteous ourselves) by ascertaining its inner reality and conforming ourselves thereto. Nietzsche called art "that sorceress expert in healing";[14] perhaps it can also be a divinity that shapes our rough-hewn ends, our looped and windowed raggednesses, if we will submit to being transformed. (Wordsworth was sure of it—that he reached the ground of his own moral being by penetrating behind phenomenal *shapes* to *forms*, even though they were the issue of a dark, invisible workmanship and the way to them led through strange fits of passion.) And what is a formula but a diminutive form—an animula, vagula, blandula—a house cat we can handle with relative safety and, in the process, get some understanding of the fiercely beautiful tiger (or is it a loose and baggy monster?)—the underlying classic form, as Blackmur calls it, "behind the forms we merely practice."[15]

This is not easy to do well and truly. Lucius Elder has demonstrated that attempts to rationalize tragedy are really its antagonists in its effort to incarnate itself;[16] likewise it is a meretricious softening when the critic gives in to the desire to solve, explain, or be reassured or comforted or cheered up. "They say miracles are past," says Lafeu the critic-commentator of *All's Well That Ends Well* (itself a sufficiently revealing title), "and we have our philosophical persons, to make modern and familiar things supernatural and causeless. Hence is it that we make trifles of terrors, ensconcing ourselves into seeming knowledge when we should submit ourselves to an unknown fear."[17] Even the tragedians themselves, under the terrific stress of their intuitions, more often than not succumb to the demands and blandishments of religious or ethical direction, heroic humanism, or the satisfying rigors of conventional aesthetics—Blackmur's executive form, most commonly dramatic. Murray Krieger has put it definitively:

> But fearful and even demoniac in its revelations, the [tragic] vision needed the ultimate soothing power of the aesthetic form which contained it—of tragedy itself—in order to preserve for the world a sanity which the vision itself denied.[18]

But, besides unwarrantedly identifying the thing itself with its container, this too has its dangers, of distortion or attenuation.[19] The fallacy of mere containment ranges from E. T. Owen's remark that for the Greeks tragedy was such in virtue of its technical form, through what George Steiner calls "a final elegance of action, achieved at the expense of life," to the dispiriting everyday spectacle of the TV news announcer packaging his nuggets of personal and political disaster, corruption, and sudden death within the time and space (Aristotelean unities!) dictated by the commercials which precede and follow—and using the same "sincere" school-of-elocution tone of voice for both.[20]

Nevertheless, the formalist approach (as we shall see later, even "Open Form" is a formal view) has perhaps the best chance to succeed in grasping the hard core of tragedy. *Its* besetting sin is the emptying out of all content to contain the underlying form within, or transmute it into, the new, self-sufficient forms: Francis Ferguson's paradigm of a dramatic action—purpose, passion, perception—is nicely consonant with tragedy; but it can also serve for any other art-vision.[21] Tragedy does have a subject matter and a point of view; its classic form has to do with some idea of good and evil, innocence and guilt, and the just, that is, the true, relation between them. So, in trying to study (not just absorb) tragedy, we began to look for evidence, testimony, of the form behind or within the forms.

And it began to work, in a kind of dialectic. The stuff itself, the tragic pieces, yielded formulas or parts of them—momentary crystallizations, epitomes, epigraphs of themselves. These began to display a family likeness, at first within the single piece and then as echoes and cross-references to others of the same author, then (often surprisingly) from a great variety of writings. The sentiment was encountered again and again; the form (sometimes the very rhythm) was iterative. A persistent idea began to emerge and became tentatively firm. Then, as one reread the works with the formulas in the back of one's mind, new or modified interpretations began to spring up, often demanding drastic modifications of former understanding. These new readings would then feed back into the formulas, sharpening or refining or correcting them too. As I continued to teach courses in tragedy and Shakespeare and in Renaissance drama and in Renaissance nondramatic literature (sometimes concurrently, sometimes alternately), this fruitful dialectic kept on; and gradually something like a basic minimum, a hard-core formulaic touchstone, seemed to be shaping up in the alembic.[22]

My working formula came out thus: Tragedy is consumated when the dream of innocence is confronted by the fact of guilt, and acquiesces therein.[23] It tried to be untendentious, neutral, uncommitted to any importation of meaning or value which might contaminate it as the paradigm of an action: descriptive, not prescriptive. But it is still ineluctably descriptive of *something*—not just any thesis, antithesis, and synthesis. The dream, the plus value, is of something; so is the fact, the negative: only the cancelling out through equation can be usefully kept to a relative emptiness of value-content—to a state or condition rather than a substance.

The ideal of this kind of thing, I suppose, is the physicists' "objective" statement that there exists a mirror world of antimatter on the other side, as it were, of the world of matter. Teilhard de Chardin (who claims that *The Phenomenon of Man* must be read "purely and simply as a scientific treatise") begins by describing this basic complexity in "the stuff of the universe": "there is necessarily a *double aspect to its structure* . . . coextensive with their Without, there is a Within to things." But these austere and pure intuitions are quickly undermined: Teilhard very soon begins to speak in terms of value. ("Every synthesis costs something." "Nothing is constructed except at the price of an equivalent destruction.") He goes on into consciousness, hominisation, society, and the "hyperpersonal"; his appendix provides a quick view of what he calls "the negative of the photograph," loaded with words like *evil* and *wickedness*, "which inevitably seep out through every nook and cranny, through every joint and sinew" of his system.[24] A. N. Whitehead also employs our tune and rhythm: "At the heart of the nature of things, there are always the dream of youth and the harvest of tragedy." But this scientist is confessedly pressing on the bounds of his system (the book is called *Adventures of Ideas*), and he arrives ultimately at the affective conclusion: "The Adventure of the Universe starts with the dream and reaps tragic Beauty. This is the secret of the union of Zest with Peace:—That the suffering attains its end in a Harmony of Harmonies."[25]

Robert Louis Stevenson in *Pulvis et Umbra* endowed all creatures, even the lowly ant, with the tragic sense: "in his ordered polities and rigorous justice we see confessed the law of duty and the fact of individual sin . . . this desire of well-doing and this doom of frailty runs through all the grades of life." But he too has his *yet:* "What a monstrous specter is this man, the disease of the agglutinated dust, . . . and yet . . . known as his fellows know him, how surprising are his attributes!" He ends his truly bleak picture with an imprecatory *Let it be* and a hortatory *Surely!*[26]

Perhaps the closest approximation to the formula I found is Ralegh's near the end of the *History of the World:* "It is therefore Death alone [not even God] that can suddenly make man to know himself. He holds a glass before the eyes of the most beautiful, and makes them see therein their deformity and rottenness, and they acknowledge it."[27] It is all there: the dream, the fact, the connection between them, and the winning out, the prevailing, of the bad over the good. But this insight too is embalmed, as it were, in a larger context, and we remember that even the Ralegh who could write "The Lie" had other encompassing visions, beyond the tragic. (He could blinker his sudden vision of the unknowability of historical truth by remarks like: ". . . for it is not to be feared that time should run backward and, by restoring the things themselves to knowledge, make our conjectures ridiculous.")

Shakespeare has an enormous gamut here; one hardly knows which is the theme and which the variation, or the obverse. From *Measure for Measure* we pick up the Duke's "Be absolute for death" speech, as a refrain of Ralegh's; it ends somewhat like our formula: "What's yet in this That bears the name of life? Yet in this life lie hid more thousand deaths. Yet death we fear, that makes these odds all even." And this is antiphonal to Claudio's "Our natures do pursue, Like rats that ravin down their proper bane, A thirsty evil, and when we drink we die." Isabella contributes her strain: 'But man, proud man, drest in a little brief authority, Most ignorant where he's most assured, His glassy essence, like an angry ape, Plays such fantastic tricks before high Heaven As make the angels weep." There is Hotspur's "But thought's the slave of life, and life's Time's fool, and Time, that takes survey of all the world, Must have a stop." Hamlet: "Though I am native here And to the manner born, it is a custom More honoured in the breach than the observance . . . indeed it takes From our achievement, though performed at height, The pith and marrow of our attribute." "The dram of eale Doth all the noble substance often dout To his own scandal." "We fat all creatures else to fat us, and we fat ourselves for maggots." Or a lyrical expansion and variation, Gertrude on Ophelia's death:

> Her clothes spread wide
> And mermaidlike awhile they bore her up—
> Which time she chanted snatches of old tunes,
> As one incapable of her own distress,
> Or like a creature native and indued
> Unto that element.   But long it could not be
> Till that her garments, heavy with their drink,
> Pulled the poor wretch from her melodious lay
> To muddy death.

Troilus in the midst of wooing Cressida (who has asked whether there be nothing monstrous in Cupid's pageant): "This is the monstruosity of love, lady, that the will is infinite and the execution confined, that desire is boundless and the act a slave to limit." There is Iago, confounding fair and foul, Divinity of Hell:

> And what's he then that says I play the villain?
> When this advice is free I give and honest,

Probal to thinking, and indeed the course
To win the Moor again? She's framed as fruitful
As the free elements
. . .
So will I turn her virtue into pitch,
And out of her own goodness make the net
That shall enmesh them all.

Sometimes Shakespeare too softens it and indeed turns it on itself, as a kind of inverse oxymoron: the Second Lord in *All's Well* chants (like the strophe of a chorus): "as in the common course of all treasons we still see them reveal themselves till they attain to their abhorred ends, so he that in this action contrives against his own nobility, in his proper stream o'erflows himself." The First Lord replies, toning it down: "The web of our life is of a mingled yarn, good and ill together. Our virtues would be proud if our faults whipped them not, and our crimes would despair if they were not cherished by our virtues." The best texts, of course, are in *King Lear;* they will be put to use in a later chapter.

To put an arbitrary stop to this round, this tragic fugue, let us hear the sphinx-like melody from a few moderns. Eliot struck in early: "Between the idea and the reality. . . . Between the desire and the spasm, falls the Shadow."[28] But he soon moved into his own forms of musical resolution. One of the formulations I have found most useful is thrown up in the middle of Arthur Koestler's second essay on the Yogi-Commissar antinomy: "The freedom of the whole is the destiny of the part: the only way to comprehend destiny is to comprehend one's partness."[29] But having achieved this clear and neat nugget, this tragic world in a nutshell, he cannot be bounded in it and hastily backs away from the implications of his *only;* and later modulates through a fascinated playing with the consequences of his intuition, in *Insight and Outlook,* to the wistfulness of *The Age of Longing.*[30] Camus hits it off repeatedly in the early essays of *The Myth of Sisyphus:* "The absurd is born of this confrontation between the human need and the unreasonable silence of the world." "The irrational, the human nostalgia, and the absurd that is born of their encounter." "My appetite for the absolute and for unity and the impossibility of reducing this world to a rational and reasonable principle—I also know that I cannot reconcile them." But, again, his myth of Sisyphus itself is humanistically, willfully assertive: "One must," he says, "imagine Sisyphus happy." (*Must*, indeed; *Surely*, said Stevenson.)[31] Conrad's text is interesting here too, because it is self-conscious and explicit in reversing the terms of the formula:

> The romantic feeling of reality was in me an inborn faculty. This in itself may be a curse, but, when disciplined by a sense of personal responsibility and a recognition of the hard facts of existence shared with the rest of mankind, becomes but a point of view from which the very shadows of life appear endowed with an internal glow. And such romanticism is not a sin. It is none the worse for the knowledge of truth. It only tries to make the best of it, hard as it may be; and in this hardness discovers a certain aspect of beauty.[32]

He too seems to be provoked into protesting more than the situation requires.

Finally, we can perhaps best end this selection of whistlers against the haunting refrain from the graveyard with Yeats, who comes into our subject from many entrances: poet, tragedian, autobiographer, critic, visionary. "But is there any comfort to be found? Man is in love and loves what vanishes, What more is there to say?" "We begin to live when we have conceived life as tragedy." "Today I add to that first conviction, to that first desire for unity, this other conviction . . . only the greatest obstacle that can be contemplated without despair rouses the will to full intensity." "A conviction that we should satirize rather than praise, that original virtue arises from the discovery of evil." "I came back for Hamlet at the graveside: there my delight always begins anew." Henry V. "fails in the end, as all men great and little fail in Shakespeare," who "spoke all tales with tragic irony." These have the gnomic ring of the poet, something of the tune; but even here, and often right

next to the striking intuition, there is an opposite and overpower-
ing assertion, that of one of the last romantics: "For art is a revela-
tion, and not a criticism"; tragic art is "an art of the flood . . .
passionate art, the drowner of dykes . . . alluring us almost to the
intensity of trance." He always hurries on, driven, no doubt, by
that hankering after comfort we all are subject to, to the transcendence, to "athletic joy," to his own vision of good that over-
powers his vision of evil.[33] B. L. Reid summarizes it well for us,
out of *Lapis Lazuli:* Yeats "confesses the conventional negative
tragic facts of man's condition, then scoffs at those satisfied to find
that negative conclusive; he virtually redefines dramatic tragedy
. . . by an overmastering extension of tragic reconciliation into a
kind of triumphant hilarity; finally, he passionately reasserts the
humanistic immunity of man to destiny."[34]

Boom, boomelay, boom—bang the drums loud and fast, to
drown out the slow, lowly rhythm; ring out the bells wildly, that
the tolling for thee and me might be unheard. The still, sad music,
however, the strain with the dying fall, is built into the underlying
classic form of tragedy and will be back to nag at an ear pitched to
the tragic sense when the tumult and the shouting have died.

III

This hammering away at the fragile metaphor of the tragic
tune—no doubt having cracked the wind of the poor phrase in
the process—has been in the interest of emphasizing the importance
of the word *acquiesce* in my own formula, as a necessary and salu-
tary neutral word to counterbalance the affective content residual
in *dream of innocence* and *fact of guilt*. Our lusting after comfort—in the form of either intellectual understanding or emotional
satisfaction—moves us irresistibly toward words like *acceptance,
agreement, reconciliation,* even *Christian resignation, hope, salvation.* But this, while valid for theology or even humanistic ethics,
is illegitimately imported into basic or hard-core tragedy.[35] Again,

Yeats can be the spokesman. He reportedly remarked to John Sparrow, "The tragedy of sexual intercourse is in the perpetual virginity of the soul." His Crazy Jane won't leave it at that: "But love has pitched his mansion in The place of excrement; For nothing can be sole or whole That has not been rent." Wholeness is the end product, not the rending.[36] The tough tragic way of putting it is rather, as Teilhard de Chardin does when he comes back to his photographic negative, "There are no summits without abysses."[37] Even this, of course, does not escape contamination: *summit* and *abyss* are loaded words; but it approaches more nearly the desideratum of the merely descriptive by using the impersonal and almost algebraic *there are* and the relatively colorless *without* instead of the hope or promise embedded in Yeats's *can be* or the aprioristic, *post-hoc-ergo-propter-hoc* insinuation of his *has been.* Shakespeare's "So foul a sky clears not without a storm" (from that most sardonic of the Histories, *King John*; the sentence was Conrad's epigraph for *Nostromo*) comes close to assigning the priorities rightly: the *clearing* is involved in and hedged by the foulness and the storm, and its emergence is rendered doubtful by the insistence of *so* and the double negative of *not without.*[38] My *acquiesce* too has accretions of acceptance, approval, agreement, and so on, but I would like to think that we can insist on root meanings in a formula, can maintain that the essence of the tragic result is merely a state of *being at rest*, of "being quiet in the face of the mystery brought to epiphany."[39]

There is place here for one or two more of the signs, the stigmata of what I would term "hard" tragedy: something of what might be behind William James's calling success the "bitch-goddess"[40] and something of what might be lurking under the smiling mask of poetic justice. Our epigraph here is: For every winner there must be at least one loser. This is a hard saying, especially in our "untragic" American culture, which is predicated on success as the proof of virtue and the pursuit of happiness as an unalienable right of all men, its achievement part of a self-evident truth; but it is frighteningly easy to point out that these imperial figures of speech are bare, if not indeed forked, creatures. The words themselves arouse derisive echoes: the hound pursues the hare, surely not for the hare's happiness. "Our natures do pursue, Like rats that ravin down their proper bane, A thirsty evil." Erich Frank can say, "The opportunities of life are limited, and whatever we own we are bound to have taken away from others."[41] Each occupation, we say innocently, has its legitimate pursuits—fine word, *legitimate;* fine word, *pursuit.*

In the world of phenomena, the physicists again start us off with a deceptively easy and old-fashioned description of reality: for every action there is an equal and opposite reaction. This is well, we say; it is neat, and accounts for everything without messy left-overs—or, if anything, there is an increment, a bonus, something for nothing; *reculer pour mieux sauter;* Operation Bootstrap; perpetual one-upmanship. But these same physicists tell us about entropy, about the notorious Second Law of Thermodynamics, that the universe is running down.[42] Teilhard de Chardin again can be our language mediator: "As though regulated by a sort of quantum law, the energies of life seem unable to spread in one region or take on a new form except at the expense of a lowering elsewhere . . . obeying a law from which nothing in the past has been exempt, evil may go on growing alongside good, and it too may attain its paroxysm at the end in some specifically new form." "Nature," R. Y. Hathorn points out, "is a kind of balanced chaos in which things devour and obliterate one another." "Every exercise of freedom," says E. L. B. Cherbonnier, "involves the individual in a decision for some particular aspect of reality at the expense of another." "Wherever there is a human society, there are terrible injustices," says Wyndham Lewis. "Power tends to corrupt, and absolute power corrupts absolutely."[43] There isn't enough to go around. The haves and the have-nots. Hamlet's liberty, says King Claudius, "is full of threats to all, To you yourself, to us, to everyone." "Condition!" exclaims Aufidius in *Coriolanus.* "What good condition can a treaty find I' the part that is at mercy?" There are no clean revolutions. As Oscar Mandel puts it, the social upheaval itself is a tragic purpose: "Call it the longing for social justice, though a better name for it is the natural greed of the dispossessed."[44]

Robert Warshow packs into an essay ("The Gangster as Tragic Hero") all the brutal ingredients of what might be called culture-success and shows that such success carries its own calculus of failure: "one is *punished* for success."[45] And the notion persists as we move from economics and politics and ethics into areas where we might hope that refinement would bring some mitigation. I have cited Nietzsche on art as healer, and we may eventually come back to this for our own consolation, but meantime there is plenty of testimony that, as Mandel puts it, "by a strange parasitism . . . all the arts seem to depend in large measure upon human suffering."[46] Leslie Fiedler, in "No! in Thunder!" although he too (like Camus and Benn) ends up by redeeming the negativist from nihilism by awarding him the delight of giving form and the paradoxical positivism of affirming the void, has argued most powerfully that "the form of a book represents either a moral critique of man and society, or a moral surrender," and that "insofar as a work of art is, as art, successful, it performs a negative critical function; for the irony of art in the human situation" lies in the fact that "the image of man in art . . .—precisely when it is most magnificently portrayed—is the image of failure. There is no way out."[47]

What, though, of the realm of the spirit? Here I do not mean the spirit of man, the nobility of human aspiration and heroism and altruism, for the fester in the heart of *that* lily is all too easily visible; even on the "moral" plane we are soon confronted by the disconcerting consideration, as Laurence Lerner points out, that "the value of forgiveness entails not being able to extend it to everyone." Reinhold Niebuhr time and again has wrestled with the knowledge that not only are cultural and rational and aesthetic structures all Towers of Babble, but every human enterprise, *particularly* the highest and noblest, is contaminated by an inescapable pride; that "the highest expression of human spirituality, therefore, contains also the subtlest form of human sin." "Man contradicts himself within the terms of his true essence." John Jones finds the same for the Greeks: "The palpitating unease of Greek Tragedy springs from a world in which to be sure your hands are clean is to convict yourself of hubris."[48] Dream of innocence, fact of guilt. It is not merely a hard choice, like that of the rich young man: if you want to win your soul you must lose the world; it is the chance, rather the likelihood, nay indeed the built-in certainty, that taking thought, acting spiritually, will bring pride, that deadliest of all the mortal sins. Peace is war. Success is failure. Only the victor can afford to be magnanimous; and even he who wins loses.

And where, we hunger with Job, is the justice of all this? But there is no justice; might makes right; there is "at the best," as Stevenson says, "a municipal fitness." Yet something here fascinates and even cajoles us into a feeling of satisfaction, of what I think is a false security. "We have our philosophical persons, to make modern and familiar things supernatural and causeless." We leap to statistical conclusions, Euclidean beauties, Aristotelean explanations, Hegelian syntheses, Nietzschean rhapsodies. And in the realm of literature we invoke, lightheartedly enough, another terrible goddess, Poetic Justice. But a strict, or hard, approach will show the overweening temerity of this application for a sinecure in Zion in at least two ways. True "poetic" justice is the achievement and placement of *le mot juste*—and the exact word is more likely to be devastating, or at least exacting, than to be consoling. And in the looser sense (Rymer's, who probably coined the term in 1678), the tying in of poetic justice with "the observance of the constant order of law of nature and of Providence"[49] sends us back with the tragic poets to our uneasy scrutiny of both Nature and Providence: what indeed are *their* notions and modes of justice?

The first consideration, of equity among words, is too complex and ultimately too mysterious to do very much with here; I will only point to a few of the possibilities which are somewhat in line with our theme of formula and paradigm.[50] We need go no further into the scientific study of language than such intermediary explorers as William Empson, with his demonstration of the ambiguities and booby traps built into complex words (and most words—even innocuous-seeming *ifs* and *ands*—can be vastly complex); or W. Clemen and then E. A. Armstrong, who carried us more deeply into the murky unconscious of Shakespeare's imagination from the orderly tabulation of Caroline Spurgeon's imagery count; or M. M. Mahood's investigation into Shakespeare's punning: there is enough even here to set up a theory of the tragic view in terms of *poetic* "justness." Miss Mahood insists that Shakespeare "plays with verbal meanings, not because the rhetoricians approve of wordplay, but because his imagination as a poet works through puns," that "no rhetorical principle of 'decorum' holds Shakespeare back or thrusts him towards his fatal Cleopatra."[51] But merely leafing through Sr. Miriam Joseph's compilation of the remarks of the rhetoricians themselves as they *describe* the figures, schemes, and tropes of language (which are "derived from the topics and forms of logic") strikes one with the ingrained duplicity of poetry. And, in spite of the apparent enmity between logic, the instrument of reason, and tragedy, it is really only ethic that is the incompatible: a logical extreme is usually (by virtue of the mystery inherent in the *logos*) a logical absurdity; and hence eminently tragic.[52] For example: the logician Raphe Lever remarks that "no man is saide to knowe anye thing throughly afore he know the causes thereof." Sr. Miriam Joseph supplies the gloss, "this is pre-eminently true of the formal cause," for "the formal cause is that which makes a thing to be what it is"; yet, Abraham Fraunce is forced to conclude, "the naturall and internall forms of things be hardly either known and understood, or expressed and made plaine . . . So that for the most part things be not knowne."[53] Antithesis, distinction, disjunction, debate, equivocation, dilemma; argument, disputation, sophistry, persuasion; the syllogism, which slides inexorably towards the equivocal (with the fourth-term fallacy and the en-

thymeme) as its conclusion follows the weaker premise—the rhetoricians were fascinated with these dubious formulas of expression
to the virtual exclusion of straightforward ones. They denounce, in
passing, what are called "vices" of language and reasoning, but it is
often difficult to distinguish the proper use from the abuse (Putten-
ham, for example, hardly gets out of the difficulty by calling figu-
rative language "good abuse"): all are testimonials to the basic
contingency of the world and men, to a necessary skepticism about
man's ability to know reality or to *speak* it. God's own Word can
be transmitted to men, apparently, only in parables and oracles; not
only recognizably fiendish witches are equivocators and word-
jugglers, but Apollo himself, the tutelary deity of western man
rationis capax from Herodotus to late Shakespeare (*The Winter's
Tale*), speaks in ambiguities and riddles. "To doubt the real relationship between name and nominee," Miss Mahood points out,
"between a word and the thing it signified, was to shake the whole
structure of Elizabethan thought and society."[54] But the poets had
been doing this from the beginning, "making" their "golden"
worlds out of allay; apparently only the loaded word can ade-
quately serve poetic justness.

Aristotle's notion of *hamartia*, most commonly rendered as
"tragic flaw," has done much harm to rigorous theory—introducing criteria of problem-solving and explanation and the condign
punishment important to ethicians and social engineers; but it can
help us to recognize the hard tragic even in what Donald Davie has
called the "articulate energy" of grammar and syntax, not to mention the enormous possibilities for shading one's meaning demonstrated by the suprasegmental linguisticians.[55] Think first of the
inconsistencies, the imprecisions, in any language system: ambiguous reference, swinging modifiers, reflexives, ethical datives and/or
intensives, subjective and/or objective genitives, restrictive-nonre-
strictive punctuation, unanalyzable and untranslatable packages of
meaning in idiomatic expressions, and the like. Think of the reser-
vations and timebombs embedded in every complex sentence: the

much desired simple assertion, the Yea or Nay communication, bristling with subjunctives, disjunctives, adversatives, qualifications, restrictions, conditions; takings-back and Indian-givings. Remember the fatal Cleopatra, who herself thrived on variety and riggishness:

> I do not like "But yet," it does allay
> The good precedence, fie upon "But yet,"
> "But yet" is as a gaoler to bring forth
> Some monstrous malefactor.[56]

"Much virtue in 'If,'" Shakespeare has Touchstone humorously point out; but we do not find much comfort in it when it is the sign of a condition contrary to fact or desire. *And* as a connective—surely, we think, the safest, most joyous additive, producer of bonuses—turns out to be highly loaded. *And yet* is almost as bad as *but yet;* there are mysterious and sinister identities of usage between *and* and *if.*[57]

But the special tragic tune comes in with those locutions and syntactical patterns which display the inevitable built-in hopelessness of human endeavor; in which the reflexives and identificatives predominate: *oneself, one's proper, one's own; the same, the very, the more . . . the more, just as, even as, at once with;* the relative of expectation, frustrated (Davie cites the special poignancy of Camillus's fate in Sackville's *Buckingham*, "banisht by them whom he did thus detbind," as a little tragic plot of syntax, with the hinge on the relative pronoun).[58] "Tis now the very witching time of night"—very, veritable, true, and deadly.[59] The poets, of course, are most resourceful and insistent in using these baleful economies of language and syntax and rhythm, but the sober, earnest critics too fall into them again and again—you may recall them in the few I have quoted from just now—even as they try patiently and discursively to separate out, to analyze, the tragic nexus, and so unarm the bomb, as it were. (What have *I* just written: *"Even as* they. . . .") Here are a few more. Erich Frank, illustrating Sartre: "The higher developed the moral consciousness of the individual, the more seriously he takes his moral obligations, the more clearly he will understand the inevitability of guilt in the very process of perfecting himself." Rheinhold Niebuhr: "The seed of death was in the very perfection of life of [the 13th century]. The Empire State building was completed just as the great depression came upon us. ... The new League of Nations building in Geneva was completed just in time to hear the Emperor of Abyssinia's vain plea for justice from the League." Oscar Mandel: "At the point of the perfect 'organization of human resources' comes the death of the soul." "Not only the aesthetic experience, but love and pity and courage and admiration imply the existence of evil." "Death is bitter only because life was good." Elder: "Precisely those things which make personality worth having: hope and aspiration, and the power to reorganize the world from within, are just the things man cannot have and yet live."[60] We are such smiling rogues as Kent denounces, who often try to bite the holy cords atwain which are too intrinse to unloose; we mortal wretches, poor venomous, angry fools, with our sharp teeth try to untie the knot intrinsicate of the life of tragedy, but the fatal Cleopatra of involved language escapes to call us asses unpolicied; the worm's an odd worm, and will do his kind. The beguiling notion of *hamartia*, of poetic justice, turns out to be our proper bane.

When we find ourselves in this trap of our own devising—namely, that, as Hathorn points out, "naturalistic thought is . . . necessarily equational thought" (and is not an equation the penultimate form of zero, not unity?)—we commonly seek refuge in the opposite kind, "transcendental thought."[61] And so do the poets. Tragedy worthy of the name *is* "an affair with the gods," an attempt to "show the heavens more just"—and here again, it seems, there is a soft and a hard form to be encountered. No one has ever seen, much less bespoken, tragedy bare: certainly not the critics and interpreters, who often want to use its power in the interests of buttressing some other vision of life—religion or liberal humanism or ethics or philosophy or drama-aesthetics.[62] The interesting thing is that the tragedians themselves, even those who spend their artistic lives grappling with its dark angel, never quite dare or are able to look it in the face and utter its ineffable name. On earth, things cancel out each other; all is vanity:

> If that the heavens do not their visible spirits
> Send quickly down to tame these vilde offenses,
> It will come,
> Humanity must perforce prey on itself,
> Like monsters of the deep.[63]

Astraea has left the world in disgust; but surely, one says, she has retired to her own clear state of blessedness and justness—and if, through that piety which the tragic hero has and maintains toward the transcendental, we can participate in it, we too can be saved. This is the leap of faith (or the Platonic Ladder, or the Great Chain of Being), which is based on two assumptions, or reasons of the heart: that the ways of God are just, and that they can be justified to man; that is, that God's justice is of the same kind as our notions of equity, compensation, increment even if it has to be earned. But this is hankering again, and the hard tragic view undermines it whenever we relax our vigilance and let the troll emerge from under the bridge. In spite of Aristotle's choice of *Oedipus Tyrannos* as his paradigm for *hamartia*, we have at length come to realize that Oedipus sins, is guilty, not in *doing* what he is fated to do, but in acquiring the knowledge of the deeds (this is the action of the play)—a kind of knowledge which is appropriate to, endurable by, compatible with the innocence of, only the gods. There is, of course, an analogue with Adam's acquisition of the knowledge of good and evil, which only God can contain without bursting and corruption.

In specifically religious contexts, the scandal of God's dealings with man is patent enough and has been agonized over by theologians and moralists, in the manner of the *Book of Job*, interminably and indeterminately enough; that the debate should have produced that astonishing performance, Jung's *Answer to Job,* is sufficient testimony for us here of its deep tragic recalcitrancy.[64] My point (and indeed one of Jung's) is that Job does not get satisfaction, he gets God's kind of Justice; and he does not assent to the judgment, or endorse it, or rejoice in it, he simply acquiesces. His questioning is stilled, but his question is not answered.[65] The ways of God, for any tragic-minded person, are a scandal to Hebrews and a stumbling block to Greeks. I have delivered myself before on Christianity and tragedy[66] and will invoke it here only to note that even in asserting eternal Providence and its transcendency I was confronted with the many paradoxes in the *New* Testament—paradoxes which are kept from being tragic dilemmas only by the exercise of the theological virtues. Hard tragedy is lurking underneath all the time; its rocky spikes keep thrusting up into our cleared and cultivated fields.[67] Jung points to one of these stones, which we have found so scandalously immovable that we have perforce declared it to be bread, when he describes the vicarious atonement of Christ as "the strange fact that the God of goodness is so unforgiving that he can only be appeased by a human sacrifice!"[68] Blessed are they who hunger and thirst after righteousness, for they shall be filled; theirs is the kingdom of heaven. But it is a blessedness much incommensurate with our vision of good, our dream of innocence. We have prettified the Christ into "gentle Jesus, meek and mild," in order, I suspect, to avoid having to notice the rocks in the fair field of the Gospels. We say glibly, with those "vain repetitions" Christ specifically warned against, The Lord's Prayer; but what is involved in this communion between us children and the Father who is in heaven? (Just before Christ taught his disciples the prayer, He gave another cryptic, formulaic admonition: "Be ye therefore perfect, even as your Father who is in Heaven is perfect." This is a powerful thought, not to be embarked upon but in fear and trembling.) When the Paternoster is prayed in the Catholic Mass, it is introduced by the formula, "*Warned* by saving precepts, and *formed* by divine institution, we *dare* to say, Our Father. . . ."

And if we think about it, great daring indeed is called for to ask that the Kingdom of Heaven come on earth, that God's will should be done here in the same manner as there, that God's forgiveness of our debts to Him (which are incalculable) should be commensurate with our ability (small enough: remember, winners and losers) to equalize the possession of goods. The last two petitions of The Lord's Prayer ("And lead us not into temptation, but deliver us from evil") seem to recognize the danger in such an audacious invocation of judgment: it has been pointed out that a more accurate version of the first would be "drag us not to the trial," and the evil we need deliverance from is seen, by virtue of the *and-but* connectives, to lie in that very confrontation, that measuring-up to perfection, which we have invoked.[69] One can find even here, in The Lord's Prayer, an under-the-surface analogue to our formula: the dream of innocence (of participating in God's holiness and His kingdom on earth) is confronted by the fact of guilt (by way of the idea of debt, the realization that such participation is unbearable, for the Kingdom is God's, and His is the power and the glory), and this admission is one of failure. We ask for deliverance, to be let off; and Amen, So be it, is the acquiescence. I present this little exercise (*salva reverentia*) as evidence of the great potency and penetrating quality of the hard tragic sense, and its classic, lapidary form.

IV

Let us go to one more enterprise in theodicy for another view of tragic practice and theory: Aeschylus's *Oresteia*.[70] William Arrowsmith came forward, a few years ago, with an essay "The Criticism of Greek Tragedy," in which he magisterially cuts through the palimpsest of critical additives which have damped down what he calls the turbulence at the heart of tragedy: in *Antigone*, if we look well, "we cannot help seeing and reporting . . . the real disorder (but also the tragic symmetry) of a world where the living of love

involves the denial of love elsewhere"; Euripides (whom, one re-
members, even Aristotle called the most tragic of the poets), except
in those romantic plays in which necessity is suspended, is shown
to move toward "tragedy of total turbulence."[71] And when Arrowsmith comes to Aeschylus he places *Agamemnon* squarely in
our context: "moral action is obscured and prevented by a deep
discord in the nature of things . . . a nightmare of justice in which
the assertion of any right involves a further wrong . . . choices are
irreparably clouded by inconsistency and discord among the gods."
Agamemnon and Clytemnestra are jointly responsible, accomplices,
with the gods and destiny for destruction and murder; there is
anomaly, contradiction, moral irresponsibility on earth *and* in
heaven: here indeed is god's kingdom come. Arrowsmith suggests
that "we can almost hear Aeschylus saying between the lines, 'how
can we expect men to be better than gods?' and concludes with
'the real complexity and enormous moral turbulence of the *Oresteia.*' " But (in his turn, as critic) Arrowsmith has moved on from
these hard cores to describe the whole trilogy as being about "nothing less than the discovery of wisdom under the yoke of awful
necessity," and even while on *Agamemnon* he explains the rocky
intuitions away by recourse to that old Aristoteleanism, *dramatic*
necessity: "How else, dramatically speaking, could Aeschylus have
shown us his gradual progress toward the light? For the light requires a darkness to dispel, and the darkness of the *Agamemnon* is
a deliberately constructed one. . . ."[72]

I would read it rather differently. Aeschylus's real tragic vision,
the real appalling intuition, what Mandel calls "the original config-
uration," *is* of darkness.[73] (We remember that for another theodicy
"in the beginning" there was darkness, and light came into being by
fiat. All subjunctives are basically hortatory or wishful: I want,
would like, feel the lack of, light; so Let it be.) Freud has told us
that "the goal of all life is death, for the inanimate was there before
the animate"[74]—Thanatos before Eros. Chaos and Old Night, the
chthonic Furies, even Spenser's Mutabilitie, *were*, first; the Olym-

pians, the Eumenides (our goddesses), Zeus our Father—these are the constructs, the wish fulfillments, of our rationalizing minds; and Aeschylus, intuitively a tragic poet (his choric odes, especially in *Agamemnon*, enlapidate the cores), is "executively" a theologue, an Aristotelean in mind and will.

Fascinating work has been done by Owen and others in showing the real action of the *Oresteia* to lie in the meaning of words,[75] especially the normative epithets given to the powers involved: Peitho-Temptation turns into Peitho-Persuasion; Zeus Xenios (the avenger of wrongs) by way of Zeus Hagoraios (the eloquent speaker) becomes Zeus Teleios, the Fulfiller. But the older, sinister meanings remain in the euphemisms in spite of the juggling and equivocation and casuistry; word-magic never quite loses its dangerous autonomy. As Hathorn points out in connection with Euripedes's Phaedra: "*Aidos*, 'innocence,' becomes *Aidos*, 'shame,' once innocence is lost. Phaedra herself says, "if it were possible to know which to use on which occasion, we should not have the identical word for both." The Erinyes are new-baptized the Eumenides, but they have retired underground again, to be a perpetual threat to the Acropolis. Peitho will tempt again to hybris. Zeus Teleios was called upon by that name to accomplish *Clytemnestra's* prayers. It is, of course, possible, as Arrowsmith does, to regard the changes as "wonderful transfigurations that chart the progress of justice": a "metamorphosis" of Peitho from a "sinister abstraction" (rather, I would say, a hard-core, formulaic, complex word) through Clytemnestra's "coiling rhetoric as she lures Agamemnon to his doom" to "finally that patient, crucial argument by which Athena persuades the Furies."[76] I would call it a progressive weakness, a willful softening of the unendurable vision of evil. In spite of much ingenious explication (or perhaps because of it), a good many readers, including myself, find the tricky, put-up solution of Athena unconvincing, and rather shabby.[77]

And then what about the "crucial difference," as Arrowsmith calls it, between Agamemnon's and Clytemnestra's murders, on the one hand, and Orestes's, on the other—"the comparative purity of the motive"?[78] This is brought forward to somehow purify the gods, to avoid the most unwelcome necessity of indicting them. We are back at Justice, poetic and otherwise: Orestes is "concerned with the determination of justice"; Electra, Sisson claims, "like Hamlet, requires to be reassured that such vengeance would indeed be the will of heaven."[79] She tries the euphemistic method too: *"Do you mean* a bringer of retribution, *or* one who shall adjudge?"* And Orestes is backed up by Apollo and Athena (another spokesman for Zeus and patroness of the Establishment of Athens); Electra can be reassured, by the successful staging of the *kommos*, that the gods *are* fully implicated and hence responsible.[80] But the problem, the dilemma of justice itself, has not been solved by the coining of a new term. (Jones remarks, "For the outraged and judging *oikos* the vengeance-killing of Clytemnestra is both a necessity and another terrible self-wounding. . . . 'Is Orestes a deliverer—or shall I say a doom?' "[81] Here even the *both/and* strategy—usually a means of avoiding the cancelling-out of *either/or*—finds itself in the service of the dark forces.) As in *Job*, God as Vindicator is still resident in God as Redeemer.

Vindicta mihi, ego retribuam, saith the Lord. It may not be too much to see our reflexives working in this formula as definitive: "My mode of being is that of revenge"—I will repay; I am Who sees to the payment of debts, eye for eye. (The Aeschylean version, from the Chorus in *Choephoroe*, is "Let word of hate answer word of hate,' shouts Justice aloud as she exacts the debt."[82]) And hard-core tragedy grapples with the fact that you cannot tame or domesticate completely something that lives by and on vengeance. Aeschylus the theologian is always balking Aeschylus the tragedian; he proceeds, at least overtly, on the basis of the theological virtues. Another wrestler with words, Franz Kafka, went the other way, and the whole way. He early recognized that "the word 'sein' signifies in German both things: to be and to belong to Him." He too tried the fearful, desperate way of poetic justice: "If you summon it by the right word, by its right name, it will come. This is the essence of magic, which does not create but summons." But he found, as J. H. Miller points out, that the world of words "undergoes a hideous process of disintegration."[83] Aeschylus, it seems to me, failed to go the tragic distance: he created instead of summoning, and turned out something quite marvelous and enchanting and consoling. *C'est magnifique, mais ce n'est pas tragedie-en-soi.*[84]

V

Shakespeare has so many versions of tragic theodicy that one is embarrassed by the richness. Surely, we are in the presence of the "hard" variety when Hamlet says he is being punished as well punisher, that the minister of Heaven's justice must be a scourge.[85] Heaven was ordinant, he remarks, even in the revenge on Rosencrantz and Guildenstern, "not shriving time allowed"; and we remember with a qualm his sardonic glee—" 'tis most sweet," " 'tis the sport to have the enginer hoist with his own petar" (as we wince at Othello's approval of Iago's suggestion that Desdemona be strangled in the very bed she had contaminated: "the justice of it pleases—good, very good."). Not only maddened Lear calls for some of his Nature-Goddess's function, blasting and vengeance, but Albany, the reasonable man, reasserts his belief in God in terms of it: "This shows you are above, You justicers, that these our nether crimes So speedily can venge." Othello, who sees himself as a god-figure, an honorable murderer, is perhaps most devastating of all, as he—whether calmly or in rage, whether he is Olympian or his soul ensnared by demidevil Iago, the dark alter ego of this demigod—"proceeds upon just grounds." "It is the cause, it is the cause, my soul. . . . This sorrow's heavenly, It strikes where it doth love"; if Cassio is not killed, then "sweet revenge grows harsh." Othello cheers himself up, exonerates himself, at the very end by reminding his auditors that he has done the state some service by avenging it on a Turk who, because he had traduced the god-state and was malignant by virtue of being turbaned and circumcised, was no better than a dog. Othello's occupation—that is, his mode of being (and precisely that for which Desdemona loves him and thus becomes implicated too)—is war, "the big wars That make ambition virtue," the glorious employment of "mortal engines, whose rude throats The immortal Jove's dread of clamors counterfeit." Macbeth too, and Coriolanus, are Bellona's bridegrooms, worthy warriors; and their activity, their evidence of godlikeness, is memorizing Golgotha and striking with planetary malignancy. Henry V, having secured the sanction of the venal Archbishops, and identifying the treason of the conspirators with the Fall of Man, declares in effect "*Got mit uns!*" and implicates God, the God of Battles, in his crying havoc and letting loose the dogs of war: "War is His beadle, War is His vengeance." No matter how Shakespeare tries (in such plays as *The Merchant of Venice* or *Measure for Measure* or *The Winter's Tale* or *The Tempest*) to work in the Christian mitigation of justice by mercy and grace and "virtue," even by using all the casuistical and tricky means at his disposal, the root meaning of heaven-gods as cruel, capricious, treacherous, *vindictive*, sprouts up, hard and indestructible as tares amid the sustaining corn.

Lionel Abel, who has recently argued that "negative facts" do not justify pessimism as a generalized view and disallowed Schopenhauer's argument as "lacking subtlety," provides in this connection a conveniently full example of the kind of peripheral considerations that I think keep us from seeing the core of tragedy:

There are two remarks in *Lear* which relate to destiny, and they contradict each other:

> As flies to wanton boys, are we to th' gods,
> They kill us for their sport.

and

> The gods are just, and of our pleasant vices
> Make instruments to plague us.

Clearly these remarks refute each other. The difficulty of thinking that both are true is the chief problem of Shakespeare's play and prevents it from being a true tragedy. We cannot accept or be exalted by the deaths of Gloucester, Cordelia or Lear himself. There is no destiny in any of these deaths, for in a true vision of destiny, the contradiction implied by the two views that (1) the gods are wanton in their treatment of us, and (2) the gods are just in their treatment of us, would be transcended. . . . The work is simply not unified. And this is one reason it tends to be ineffective on the stage.[86]

True tragedy for Mr. Abel seems to reside in (1) *our* being exalted by deaths, (2) a transcendence of contradictions in destiny, (3) one-dimensional unity within the work, and (4) effectiveness on the stage. But the negativeness of the hard tragic form does exactly produce and require an underlying unity-in-nullity; it pulls the aspiration of such phrases as "the gods are just" to being a positive, down again to zero or even an ironic minus quantity or irrational number. For the two comments in *Lear* are not contradictory, but complementary: the "justness" of the gods is as wanton as their sport, which is a "plague" to men. Indeed, the passages (alike in pithiness, sententiousness, rhythm, formula-quality) practically say (together) that for the gods, justice, sport, wantonness, plaguing, are all the same thing. (" 'Tis the sport," said Hamlet, the scourge of God.) And what is a word like *instruments*, with its overtones of torture machines, doing in a phrase extolling the goodness of the gods? What about "pleasant vices"? Oxymoron is always the sign of complex thinking and feeling, usually ironic. And who says the remarks, and in what context? Gloucester says the first, at nearly the bottom of his skepticism and atheism, *when Edgar has come into his mind;* Edgar himself, the do-gooder, the legitimate knightly revenger, says the second, followed by "The dark and vicious place where thee he got Cost him his eyes." I find this more than a bit smug and pharasaical, in a speech to the fallen Edmund about "exchanging charity."[87] Mr. Abel reestablishes his connection with the heart of the matter when he perceives that Athaliah is "tragic— to the most eminent degree" because she is equal to God in the rigor of her *vengeance*.[88]

VI

To do tragedy justice, then, and to benefit most from its mysteriously healing properties, we should resist the impulse to hanker, to adulterate, to gloss. We should, it seems to me, resist, as Marlowe did in withholding from Faustus the saving qualification of his damnable syllogism,[89] the urge to play the trump card of faith. We should resist the temptation to plunge with Yeats into hosannahs— "Rhyme can beat a measure out of trouble, And make the daylight sweet once more"—and to say that the assertion of spirit cancels the fact of defeat. Nor should we resort to a table-turning reversal of priorities like Aldous Huxley's in *Tragedy and the Whole Truth:* "the cynicism is always heroic idealism turned neatly inside out, the irony is a kind of photographic negative of heroic romance" (remember the anti-matter scientists: which is *chiaro* and which *oscuro*?). Even Elizabeth Sewell's presentation to us of epic ("one of the greatest of postlogical disciplines," whose preoccupation is with "the structure of the universe and the place and course of man's life and death within it, its essential activity, its attachment to mythology")—which it is tempting to adopt in lieu of or as inclusive of tragedy, since its "discipline" appears to contain a more positive nucleus of activity—will not, I believe, quite enable us to concentrate on truly, and perceive accurately, the tragic logic while and as we encounter it.[90]

Though the great poets cannot lie, they do tell their tales of tragic truth in ways that match the Father of Lies in sorcery and manipulation. Eternal vigilance, then, and a willed negative capability on our own part, are required if we are to "trust the tale." Complex words do have contradictory components, and all of them are subject to constant critique and redefinition; and even our formulas, our gnomic verbal duplicities, can sometimes be turned against themselves. (In *Antony and Cleopatra*, to reverse the formula, the nightmare of guilt is confronted by the miracle of innocence, and dissolves in frustrated acquiescence; virtue, though not quite infinite, does come smiling, though with a somewhat crooked smile, from the world's great snare uncaught.) Simone Weil says that "A mind already dwells in truth when it has become capable of grasping ideas that are inexpressible because of the great number of relationships that go to make them up"—surely a tragic insight.[91] But the poet is different from the mystic, the contemplative, in that he does not and cannot *dwell:* he struggles all the time to express; and words, the arts of language, do express some of the great number of meanings.[92] The ineffable whole truth can come most nearly to expression by means of the complex word, including not excluding the tragically self-critical. We shall next try to see how Shakespeare, servant of that master-mistress of his passion the Tragic Muse, exercises his virtue as both scourge and minister.

2

Some New Readings in Shakespeare

I WANT TO SUGGEST TWO THINGS ABOUT SHAKESPEARE: that he was loyal to the hard tragic sense, and that he wrestled with its dark angel to the very end of his artist's life—wrestled like Jacob, not danced like David, before the Lord. The great watershed in approaches to Shakespeare, I suspect, beneath the myriad differences dictated by concern with technical form or cultural placement or literary history, is the divide between our desire to affirm and celebrate, and our obscurely-felt duty to investigate and criticize: O'Neill's "proud conviction" of a possible "ennobling identity" with tragedy as against Yeats's "conviction that we should satirize rather than praise." Though these two slopes do seem to converge at the top (the plays and poems themselves), they are opposed and inexorable, and one soon finds oneself taking up a somewhat precarious position on one or the other side of the mountain. For many generations the sunny side was most populated— witness Shakespeare's own intimates in the theatre, including Ben Jonson, whose epithet for him was "gentle," "Sweet Swan of

Avon!"; Francis Meres, who in 1598 could call the sonnets "sugred"; and Milton, with his "Sweetest Shakespeare, fancy's child," a native warbler whose wit "flowed" in "easy numbers." Keats gave us our next really memorable phrases—negative capability, the chameleon poet, and the "intensity" of every art, which is "capable of making all disagreeables evaporate." And, bypassing all the rationalists and the idealists and the Christian humanists, let us listen once again to the other side of Yeats, as he announces that "Our traditions [Shakespeare, of course, is prominent therein] only permit us to bless, for the arts are an extension of the beatitudes"; and "Hamlet and Lear are gay, Gaiety transfiguring all that dread."[1]

But the whirligig of time brings in his revenges, and in spite of a strong rearguard action by (let us call them) the positivists, our own age of anxiety seems to be seeing more and more of that face of Melpomene which is turned toward the harsher light of truth: she is being recognized (chiefly through her prime minister, Shakespeare) as a critical, if not altogether cankered, muse. The larger aesthetic and formal considerations which provide a home and a sanction for this view of tragedy are catered for by such persuasive demonstations as R. M. Adams's study of open form in *Strains of Discord*, Elizabeth Sewell's *The Orphic Voice*, and J. O. Perry's "Relationship of Disparate Voices in Poems."[2] Recognition of the inquiring, even skeptical spirit rampant during the High Renaissance itself—of the centrality of Montaigne, for example—has given us such corroboration of Hiram Haydn's *Counter-Renaissance* as Robert Ornstein's *Moral Vision of Jacobean Tragedy*, D. C. Allen's *Doubt's Boundless Sea*, and E. W. Talbert's *The Problem of Order*.[3] Empson's, Sr. Miriam Joseph's, and Miss Mahood's investigations into the complexity of the language arts have found helpful followers in Jonas Barish on Shakespeare's prose as well as Murray Krieger and Wilfrid Watson on the Sonnets. Jan Kott, whether or not he has persuaded anyone about Shakespeare's being *Our Contemporary* as a political dramatist, makes a forthright paraphrase of the hard tragic skeleton to be found in the dramatic poems. Perhaps the most radical exponent of Shakespeare as inquisitor is A. P. Rossiter's *Angel With Horns,* a collection of his Cambridge and Stratford Lectures on Shakespeare which, had they not been cut off by his death in 1957, might have bid fair to be a bible of this new criticism, comparable to A. C. Bradley's in his day and G. Wilson Knight's in his.[4] I want to acknowledge my debt to such critics and especially to Rossiter, and to propose his main ideas[5] as the chief mentor for a few exercises in reading tragic Shakespeare.

Negative capability—another of those gnomic, two-pronged intuitive phrases that get to the unconscious core of things. (We may, I trust, appropriate it for our purposes and only apparently distort it from Keats's ostensible meaning, knowing that he was, beneath his bravado, rather more than half in love with easeful death himself.) Keats meant mostly a kind of receptivity, of course, an all-inclusive acceptingness, openness to everything, "when a man is capable of being in uncertainties, mysteries, doubts, without any irritable reaching after fact and reason."[6] The poet who had this chameleon quality not only could absorb and reflect all colors of the moral imagination, but took as much *delight* in imagining an Iago as an Imogen. I suggest that Keats was leaping too quickly to his own quality and attributing it pre-posterously to Shakespeare, who thought of the chameleon-poet rather differently, as one that eats the air, crammed with elusive and unfulfilled promise. The master-mistress of *his* passion, he tells us in Sonnet 20, is "A man in hue, all hues *in his controlling*"; Hamlet's "dear soul" hankers for the blessedness that comes from *not* being a pipe for fortune's finger to stop at will; and in Sonnet 111 Shakespeare chides Fortune as a guilty goddess for having almost subdued his nature to what it worked in, like the dyer's hand: this is a strong infection, a plague, for being the victim of which he asks pity and will accept bitter medicine as penance toward its correction.

That Shakespeare's negative capability is something more than that of a mere unexposed panchromatic film, and indeed more than our (by now familiar) photographic negative, could be illustrated a thousand times over just by the echoing of the word *nothing* in all his plays and poems.[7] A howling nothingness comes from a mere nothing, in *King Lear*—No, no, no life; Never, never, never, never, never! "The King," says Hamlet, "is a thing—of nothing." "The quality of nothing," Gloucester points out, "hath not such need to hide itself" as Edmund exhibits; if it be nothing indeed, one has no need for spectacles. Macbeth's vision of life is a significance of nothingness; yet it is not bearably empty, but full of sound and fury. *Timon of Athens*, which has been called, in despair of fitting it into tragedy, a misanthropy, puts it at its most rigorous: "My long sickness Of health and living now begins to mend, And nothing brings me all things." *Naught* is not blank zero, but an alive and irrational quantity; it was not for nothing indeed that to the Elizabethans, and Shakespeare specifically, *naughty* was not a coy wrist-slapping epithet, but a word pregnant with the principle of negation. "How far that little candle throws his beams," remarks Portia returning to Belmont from Venice—and, if we stick to the original punctuation of a comma rather than an exclamation point, one of its meanings is "*only that* little distance"—"so shines a good deed in a *naughty* world," a world dull as night, dark as Erebus.

Shakespeare had an enormous capacity for the negative; whether this ingrained piety toward the spirit of negation was a source of felicity or a cursed spite to him, we shall never truly know, but it was his ruling passion, his particular poetic daemon. I would like to suggest a Shakespeare-as-critic who mediates tragedy-as-critique, with the plays, the dramatic poems, as critiques from the inside: exhibiting not only overt evil-versus-good but misgivings, qualms, about the vision of good itself, insistent if not irritable reachings after the infected source of the aching tooth. This gives a glimpse of a radical attempt to get inside tragedy itself, to grapple with the mystery of the evil of good. Shakespeare's conscious, willing mind and artist's craft go far enough in all conscience, in this direction, using many of the conventional and established attitudes and means: plot, characterization, rhetoric, dramatic juxtaposition, choric-character and subplot commentary, medieval-tragedy and morality-play materials, sententiae, change and shift of emphasis from his sources, and so on. Re-definition—not only by paradox, synecdoche, metaphor, oxymoron, puns, but by direct challenge and confrontation—is constantly going on.[8] He *enforces* the discrepancy, the something-rotten, the tears of things, the speed with which bright things are stained and come to confusion, confusion which makes its master-pieces of horror. But, as Rossiter has pointed out, even on this large, open level, Shakespeare had to put aside Sidneyan and Jonsonian tragic principles "in order to become a Shakespearean, not an Elizabethan, *tragedian:* a writer of genuine tragedy."[9] His version of hamartia, then, is the critique from the inside: not a flaw in an otherwise good thing, but the corruptibility of the apparent good itself. Only this can be adequate to the vision; and it *is* potentially Manichaean. But what of all the rest—the famous plenitude; the evidence of good people, good will, good motives; honor, love, obedience, troops of friends which, even if Macbeth has forfeited them, should accompany old age; the ability to forgive and expiate; the grace of Grace that can make the time free? Shakespeare has put in, or left in, a God's-plenty of such counterweights, or at least enough for the humanists and hankerers to construct their own comfortable beatitudes from. The question is *how* has he put them in, and how much control over them does he retain?

For, if the desires of man's heart are as crooked as corkscrews, the *id* of a tragic poet is all the more devious. The critics mentioned above have labored sufficiently, I trust, to get us off the old hook of the author's sincerity (Bradley, it may be remembered, repudiated as un-Shakespearean any suspicion that dramatic irony could originate as an animus of the author's[10]) by demonstrating the constant activity of wordplay and *trompe l'oeil;* "genetic puns" as well as iterative image clusters; reverse puns and even "unspoken puns," which "often carry an impossible and so negative meaning which acts as a deep shadow to make the dominant significance more brilliant." (Even this, however, displays some hankering: what constitutes dominance? How can one be sure?) Shakespeare not only normally sets us off-balance by endowing his characters with scintillating wordplay, but he often counters a character's attempt at such "with a quibble of his own." Although this almost autonomous underpower of the mind *can* work, too, in reverse, producing a critique of the critique itself, most usually it is sardonic, the debunker, the discloser of "normally-inhibited feelings." "Most of the witty word-play in Shakespeare," Miss Mahood informs us, "is either wanton or aggressive";[11] that is, we might say with Shakespeare through *Troilus and Cressida*, it displays the nasty underside of those two trumped-up heroic humanistic virtues, Love and Valor. The poet's unconscious mind is always there, working away and producing the critique, nagging, undermining; loyal to the hard tragic intuition, making us, if we read the plays fully and honestly, absorb them in all their complexity. H. D. F. Kitto acknowledges that "Shakespeare is never so *dangerous* as when he is writing poetry."[12] True, but the corollary is, When is he not? Wordplay of the order of puns (an average of 78 per play, 3000-odd in all, by Miss Mahood's count[13]) is only the most obvious, and hence perhaps the least dangerous, evidence of his poetic activity. G. Wilson Knight (like Keats, perhaps, interpolating his own willed ethos onto his ideal) says that "No one will accuse Shakespeare of lacking humour, but it is often forgotten that his humour works within the limits set by a prevailing 'high seriousness.' "[14] But how do you know? The Spirit Ironical is subversive, and very nearly a universal solvent; and even if we allow for the ostensible control of the ego, using executive form, again we should not be misled into taking the Container for the Thing Contained.

I should like to use *Macbeth* for an extended exercise in seeing and hearing Shakespearean tragic poetry. Here are six scenes which can be taken as the skeletal framework or plot of the play as a tragedy of kingship—the "royal play of Scotland." The scenes are interrelated and comment on one another by several strategies: juxtaposition; echoing of words, phrases, and expressions; structured repetition. All the scenes chiefly devote themselves to displaying the theme of battle-to-the-death-for-the-crown; and all make use of two related modes of making the kingdom come, prophecy and reporting.[15]

A c t I

scene i.—*An open place.*

Thunder and lightning. Enter three Witches.

1 *Witch.* When shall we three meet again?
　In thunder, lightning, or in rain?
2 *Witch.* When the hurlyburly's done,
　When the battle's lost and won.
3 *Witch.* That will be ere the set of sun.
1 *Witch.* Where the place?
2 *Witch.*　　　　　　Upon the heath.
3 *Witch.* There to meet with Macbeth.
1 *Witch.* I come, Graymalkin!
2 *Witch.* Paddock calls.
3 *Witch.* Anon!
All. Fair is foul, and foul is fair:
　Hover through the fog and filthy air.　　　[*Exeunt.*

scene ii.—*A camp.*

Alarum within. Enter King Duncan, Malcolm, Donalbain,
　Lenox, *with Attendants, meeting a bleeding Captain.*

Dun. What bloody man is that?　He can report,
　As seemeth by his plight, of the revolt
　The newest state.
Mal.　　　　　This is the Sergeant,
　Who, like a good and hardy soldier, fought
　'Gainst my captivity.—Hail, brave friend!
　Say to the King the knowledge of the broil,
　As thou didst leave it.

Cap.   Doubtful it stood;
   As two spent swimmers, that do cling together
   And choke their art.   The merciless Macdonwald
   (Worthy to be a rebel, for to that
   The multiplying villainies of nature
   Do swarm upon him) from the western isles
   Of Kernes and Gallowglasses is supplied;
   And Fortune, on his damned quarrel smiling,
   Show'd like a rebel's whore: but all's too weak;
   For brave Macbeth (well he deserves that name),
   Disdaining Fortune, with his brandish'd steel,
   Which smok'd with bloody execution,
   Like Valour's minion, carv'd out his passage,
   Till he fac'd the slave;
   Which ne'er shook hands, nor bade farewell to him,
   Till he unseam'd him from the nave to th' chops,
   And fix'd his head upon our battlements.

Dun. O valiant cousin! worthy gentleman!

Cap. As whence the sun 'gins his reflection,
   Shipwracking storms and direful thunders break,
   So from that spring, whence comfort seem'd to come,
   Discomfort swells.   Mark, King of Scotland, mark:
   No sooner justice had, with valour arm'd,
   Compell'd these skipping Kernes to trust their heels,
   But the Norweyan Lord, surveying vantage,
   With furbish'd arms, and new supplies of men,
   Began a fresh assault.

Dun.   Dismay'd not this
   Our captains, Macbeth and Banquo?

Cap.   Yes;
   As sparrows eagles, or the hare the lion.
   If I say sooth, I must report they were
   As cannons overcharg'd with double cracks;
   So they
   Doubly redoubled strokes upon the foe:
   Except they meant to bathe in reeking wounds,
   Or memorize another Golgotha,
   I cannot tell—
   But I am faint, my gashes cry for help.

/ 44

Dun. So well thy words become thee, as thy wounds:
  They smack of honour both.—Go, get him surgeons.

                              [*Exit Captain, attended.*

                Enter Rosse and Angus.

  Who comes here?
Mal.   The worthy Thane of Rosse.
Len. What a haste looks through his eyes!   So should he look
  That seems to speak things strange.
Rosse.   God save the King!
Dun. Whence cam'st thou, worthy Thane?
Rosse.   From Fife, great King,
  Where the Norweyan banners flout the sky,
  And fan our people cold. Norway himself,
  With terrible numbers,
  Assisted by that most disloyal traitor,
  The Thane of Cawdor, began a dismal conflict;
  Till that Bellona's bridegroom, lapp'd in proof,
  Confronted him with self-comparisons,
  Point against point, rebellious arm 'gainst arm,
  Curbing his lavish spirit: and, to conclude,
  The victory fell on us;—
Dun.   Great happiness!
Rosse. That now
  Sweno, the Norways' King, craves composition;
  Nor would we deign him burial of his men
  Till he disbursed at Saint Colme's Inch
  Ten thousand dollars to our general use.
Dun. No more that Thane of Cawdor shall deceive
  Our bosom interest.—Go pronounce his present death,
  And with his former title greet Macbeth.
Rosse. I'll see it done.
Dun. What he hath lost, noble Macbeth hath won.

                              [*Exeunt.*

Act IV

SCENE I.—*A dark cave.   In the middle, a boiling cauldron.*

      Thunder.   Enter the three Witches.

  . . . .

1 *Witch.* Round about the cauldron go;
    In the poison'd entrails throw.—
    . . . .

2 *Witch.* For a charm of powerful trouble,
    Like a hell-broth boil and bubble.
All. Double, double toil and trouble:
  Fire, burn; and, cauldron, bubble.
    . . . .

2 *Witch.* Cool it with a baboon's blood:
    Then the charm is firm and good.

        [*Enter* HECATE, *and the other three Witches.*

Hec. O, well done! I commend your pains,
    And every one shall share i' th' gains.
    And now about the cauldron sing,
    Like elves and fairies in a ring,
    Enchanting all that you put in.
    . . . .

2 *Witch.* By the pricking of my thumbs,
    Something wicked this way comes.—   [*Knocking.*
    Open, locks,
    Whoever knocks.

          Enter MACBETH.

Macb. How now, you secret, black, and midnight hags!
    What is't you do?
All.   A deed without a name.
Macb. I conjure you, by that which you profess,
    Howe'er you come to know it, answer me:
    Though you untie the winds, and let them fight
    Against the Churches; though the yesty waves
    Confound and swallow navigation up;
    Though bladed corn be lodg'd, and trees blown down;
    Though castles topple on their warders' heads;
    Though palaces, and pyramids, do slope
    Their heads to their foundations; though the treasure
    Of Nature's germens tumble all together,
    Even till destruction sicken, answer me
    To what I ask you.
1 *Witch.*   Speak.

/ 46

2. *Witch.*   Demand.

3 *Witch.*   We'll answer.

1 *Witch.* Say, if thou 'dst rather hear it from our mouths,
   Or from our masters?

Macb.   Call 'em; let me see 'em.

1 *Witch.* Pour in sow's blood, that hath eaten
   Her nine farrow; grease, that's sweaten
   From the murderer's gibbet, throw
   Into the flame.

All.   Come, high, or low;
   Thyself and office deftly show.

   Thunder. First Apparition, an armed head.

Macb. Tell me, thou unknown power,—

1 *Witch.*   He knows thy thought:
   Hear his speech, but say thou nought.

1 *App.* Macbeth! Macbeth! Macbeth! beware Macduff;
   Beware the Thane of Fife.—Dismiss me.—Enough.
                              [*Descends.*

Macb. Whate'er thou art, for thy good caution, thanks:
   Thou hast harp'd my fear aright.—But one word more:—

1 *Witch.* He will not be commanded.   Here's another,
   More potent than the first.

   Thunder. Second Apparition, a bloody child.

2 *App.* Macbeth! Macbeth! Macbeth!—

Macb. Had I three ears, I'd hear thee.

2 *App.* Be bloody, bold, and resolute: laugh to scorn
   The power of man, for none of woman born
   Shall harm Macbeth.   [*Descends.*

Macb. Then live, Macduff: what need I fear of thee?
   But yet I'll make assurance double sure,
   And take a bond of Fate: thou shalt not live;
   That I may tell pale-hearted fear it lies,
   And sleep in spite of thunder.—

   Thunder. Third Apparition, a child crowned with a tree in
              his hand.

                    What is this,
   That rises like the issue of a king;

SOME NEW READINGS IN SHAKESPEARE / 47

And wears upon his baby brow the round
And top of sovereignty?
All.   Listen, but speak not to't.
3 *App.* Be lion-mettled, proud, and take no care
Who chafes, who frets, or where conspirers are:
Macbeth shall never vanquish'd be, until
Great Birnam wood to high Dunsinane hill
Shall come against him.   [*Descends.*
Macb.   That will never be:
Who can impress the forest; bid the tree
Unfix his earth-bound root? Sweet bodements! good!
. . . .

                                —Yet my heart
Throbs to know one thing: tell me (if your art
Can tell so much), shall Banquo's issue ever
Reign in this kingdom?
. . . .

All. Show his eyes, and grieve his heart;
Come like shadows, so depart.
. . . .

1 *Witch.* That this great King may kindly say,
Our duties did his welcome pay.
                [*Music. The Witches dance, and vanish.*

A ct V

SCENE V.—*Dunsinane. Within the castle.*

Enter, with drum and colours, MACBETH, SEYTON, *and
Soldiers.*

Macb. Hang out our banners on the outward walls;
The cry is still, "They come!"
. . . .

The time has been, my senses would have cool'd
To hear a night-shriek; and my fell of hair
Would at a dismal treatise rouse, and stir,

As life were in't. I have supp'd full with horrors:
Direness, familiar to my slaughterous thoughts,
Cannot once start me.

. . . .

Life's but a walking shadow; a poor player,
That struts and frets his hour upon the stage,
And then is heard no more: it is a tale
Told by an idiot, full of sound and fury,
Signifying nothing.

Enter a Messenger.

    Thou com'st to use thy tongue; thy story quickly.
Mess. Gracious my Lord,
    I should report that which I say I saw,
    But know not how to do't.
Macb.   Well, say, sir.
Mess. As I did stand my watch upon the hill,
    I look'd toward Birnam, and anon, methought,
    The wood began to move.
Macb.   Liar, and slave!
Mess. Let me endure your wrath, if't be not so.
    Within this three mile may you see it coming;
    I say, a moving grove.
Macb.   If thou speak'st false,
    Upon the next tree shalt thou hang alive,
    Till famine cling thee: if thy speech be sooth,
    I care not if thou dost for me as much.—
    I pull in resolution; and begin
    To doubt th' equivocation of the fiend,
    That lies like truth:

. . . .

If this which he avouches does appear,
There is nor flying hence, nor tarrying here.
I 'gin to be aweary of the sun,
And wish th' estate o' th' world were now undone.—
Ring the alarum bell!—Blow, wind! come, wrack!
At least we'll die with harness on our back.

                         [*Exeunt.*

SOME NEW READINGS IN SHAKESPEARE / 49

SCENE VIII.—*Another part of the field.*

Enter MACBETH.

Macb. Why should I play the Roman fool, and die
    On mine own sword? whiles I see lives, the gashes
    Do better upon them.

Re-enter MACDUFF.

Macd.   Turn, Hell-hound, turn!
Macb. Of all men else I have avoided thee:
    But get thee back, my soul is too much charg'd
    With blood of thine already.
Macd.   I have no words;
    My voice is in my sword: thou bloodier villain
    Than terms can give thee out!
    . . . .

                  Despair thy charm;
    And let the Angel, whom thou still hast serv'd,
    Tell thee, Macduff was from his mother's womb
    Untimely ripp'd.
Macb. Accursed be that tongue that tells me so,
    For it hath cow'd my better part of man:
    And be these juggling fiends no more believ'd,
    That palter with us in a double sense;
    That keep the word of promise to our ear,
    And break it to our hope,—I'll not fight with thee.
    . . . .

    Yet I will try the last: before my body
    I throw my warlike shield: lay on, Macduff;
    And damn'd be him that first cries, "Hold, enough!"
    [*Exeunt, fighting. Alarums. Re-enter fighting, and Macbeth
    slain.*

SCENE IX.—*Within the castle.*

Retreat. Flourish. Enter, with drum and colours, MALCOLM,
    old SIWARD, ROSSE, *Thanes, and Soldiers.*

Mal. I would the friends we miss were safe arriv'd.
Siw. Some must go off; and yet, by these I see,
    So great a day as this is cheaply bought.

Mal. Macduff is missing, and your noble son.

Rosse. Your son, my Lord, has paid a soldier's debt:
    He only liv'd but till he was a man;
    The which no sooner had his prowess confirm'd,
    In the unshrinking station where he fought,
    But like a man he died.

Siw.   Then he is dead?

Rosse. Ay, and brought off the field. Your cause of sorrow
    Must not be measur'd by his worth, for then
    It hath no end.

Siw.   Had he his hurts before?

Rosse. Ay, on the front.

Siw.   Why then, God's soldier be he!
    Had I as many sons as I have hairs,
    I would not wish them to a fairer death:
    And so, his knell is knoll'd.

Mal.   He's worth more sorrow,
    And that I'll spend for him.

Siw.   He's worth no more;
    They say he parted well and paid his score:
    And so, God be with him!—Here comes newer comfort.

Re-enter MACDUFF, *with* MACBETH's *head.*

Macd. Hail, King! for so thou art.   Behold, where stands
    Th' usurper's cursed head: the time is free.
    I see thee compass'd with thy kingdom's pearl,
    That speak my salutation in their minds;
    Whose voices I desire aloud with mine,—
    Hail, King of Scotland!

All.   Hail, King of Scotland!   [*Flourish.*

Mal. We shall not spend a large expense of time,
    Before we reckon with your several loves,
    And make us even with you.   My Thanes and kinsmen,
    Henceforth be Earls; the first that ever Scotland
    In such an honour nam'd.   What's more to do,
    Which would be planted newly with the time,—
    As calling home our exil'd friends abroad,
    That fled the snares of watchful tyranny;
    Producing forth the cruel ministers
    Of this dead butcher, and his fiend-like Queen,

Who, as 'tis thought, by self and violent hands
Took off her life;—this, and what needful else
That calls upon us, by the grace of Grace,
We will perform in measure, time, and place.
So thanks to all at once, and to each one,
Whom we invite to see us crown'd at Scone.

[*Flourish. Exeunt.*

The common reading of the second and last of these scenes is
quite innocent; the animus behind such a reading is most assuredly
stated, perhaps, by C. J. Sisson, as he speaks of

> Shakespeare's insistence upon the great excellencies of Macbeth in
> the opening scenes, in which he comes close to the perfection of
> Hamlet in Ophelia's eyes. A loyal subject, a man of nobility in all
> things, a great soldier who is yet free from ruthlessness, the picture is
> almost overdrawn, and certainly has no tinge of irony. It is, with
> equal certainty, intentional that in this picture King Duncan, the
> Lords of Scotland, and the soldiers and common people are of one
> mind about Macbeth. Macbeth was a great prize, worth winning for
> his own sake as for the issues at stake in the winning.[16]

(It would be hard for me to believe that *this* almost overdrawn
critical response is not ironic, were it not for the ensuing characterization of Lady Macbeth as a tender, feminine housewife, lovingly
absorbed in her husband's pursuit of advancement; a combi-
nation of Eve and Francesca.) But every rift of the scenes is so
loaded with coiling ironies that one is staggered just trying to keep
up with them: the juxtaposition of the captain's tale with that of
the witches; the insistence indeed on the doubtfulness of everything and our inability to distinguish fair from foul, worthiness
from unworthiness, rebels and traitors from valorous, noble friends.
The battle is both lost and won, and the winners win *wha*t the losers
lose—that is, not only their titles and their worth (measured in dollars), but also "the multiplying villainies of nature." The self-comparisons are inexorably self-incriminating; in "Point against point,
rebellious arm 'gainst arm" how can we extricate the supposedly

good arm of Macbeth from the single modification of the adjective?[17] Can being Bellona's bridegroom make an honest man out of valor's minion, who is different from Fortune's whore only in being stronger? Macdonwald is merciless, Norway terrible, Cawdor dismal—these attributes are each time connected with treachery and somehow accounted for as bad because they are rebellious to the King; but Banquo and especially Macbeth smoke with bloody execution, are overcharged cannons, bathe in reeking wounds, reenact the butchery of the very Place of Skulls itself. Yet they well deserve the name of brave, valiant, worthy; like the *strange* tale of the bloody captain itself, and in exactly the same way, "they smack of honour both."

The emphasis on the telling of the story should not be lost. The bloody man can best report the battle and is invoked by Malcolm to *say it to the King.* He recognizes his role—much like that of the herald at the beginning of *Agamemnon*—to so tell the tale that, like a charm, it will enforce the desired and official interpretation of events: "Mark, King of Scotland, mark."[18] Then, also like the messenger from Troy, he finds his words getting out of control, ominously harping on the destructive, the blasphemous. He tries to use "good" comparisons—"As sparrows eagles, or the hare the lion"—but his venture into double entendre and irony frees the subversive power of language:[19] "If I say sooth [a soothsayer is in a dangerous profession] I must report that they were As cannons overcharged with double cracks." He sees what is coming, gives a hint of the kind of horrible motives he will have to attribute to the warriors ("Except they meant to bathe in reeking wounds. . . ."), and backs away from having to be the one to utter the words to the king. The king dismisses him from his function, accepting him as a worthy priest: "So well thy words become thee as thy wounds."[20] His replacement, Ross, is also well qualified for the job—"So should he look That seeks to speak things strange"—and his first words are "God save the King!" As we shall see shortly with Macbeth himself, to know and to say, in a formal, incantatory mode, the secrets

of brave and hardy soldiership, of the occupation of war, is to traf-
fic with evil spirits, to hail necromancy, like Faustus. In ordinary
political history, this would be merely machiavellism, propaganda;
Shakespeare has elected to write it as tragedy, and so has cried
"Havoc!" and let loose the demon of inquisition.

Again, the tendency of language forms, when they move toward
the comparative and gnomic and formulaic, to approximate the
root tragic situation of disaster lurking in the source of intended
good operates in the whole scene, and is given, to match the laconic
"Fair is foul, and foul is fair" of the witches, a full-dress and cen-
trally located statement:

> As whence the sun 'gins his reflection
> Shipwrecking storms and direful thunders break,
> So from that spring whence comfort seemed to come
> Discomfort swells.

Self-articulate, and half-autonomous, energy! Names are called: it
may be a coincidence that *Macbeth* rhymes with the witches'
heath, and (in a concluding benediction-like formula from the
mouth of the King!) with *death;* but all coincidences are not happy
ones, especially those dredged up from the subversive subconscious
by the metalogical sound component in words and names.

The king and the nobles and the captain, indeed, are of one mind
about Macbeth, of what he is *worth* to *them.* (I don't find the common people here, as Mr. Sisson does; *Macbeth* is a "royal play.")
Valor is the armament of justice, honor, use, *and* bosom interest.
These serve the vision of good of the establishment, the haves: prerogative is an unalienable right, loyalty the only virtue, and rebellion the cardinal sin. Reeking wounds and bloodbaths elicit from
the king joyful acclamations: Oh valiant Cousin! Worthy gentleman! Noble Macbeth! Great happiness! It is a peerless kinsman. In
scene iii, again right on the heels of the witches' prophecy to Macbeth and Banquo "To the selfsame tune and words," Duncan ratifies (through his messengers Ross and Angus) Macbeth's and his
complicity in this unearthly business:

The king hath happily received, Macbeth,
The news of thy success.   And when he reads
Thy personal venture in the rebels' fight,
His wonders and his praises do contend
Which should be thine or his.   Silenced with that,
In viewing o'er the rest o' the selfsame day,
He finds thee in the stout Norweyan ranks
Nothing afeard of what thyself didst make,
Strange images of death.

Sisson wants to see a difference between *Macbeth* and *Richard III*,[21] but on this opening score there is at least as much ground for suspecting the disinterestedness of the establishment virtues and the sanctity of kingship here as there is in "Now is the winter of our discontent Made glorious summer by this sun of York" or, for that matter, King John's "Here we have war for war and blood for blood, Controlment for controlment" or Falconbridge's "Since kings break faith upon commodity, Gain be my lord, for I will worship thee"—not to mention the whole dialectical ambivalence, as Rossiter calls it, of the history plays, the ruthless internecine dynastic bloodletting of which Shakespeare found patriotically chronicled in Holinshed, whence also came the materials for *Macbeth*.[22]

I submit that we should be prepared, by this opening scene, for finding that all the Scots nobility are implicated in confusion's masterpiece. There is something rotten in the state of Scotland, and it isn't only the Cawdors who have sharked up a list of lawless resolutes: Macbeth is the instrument of death; he is the King's most worthy gentleman; God must save the King; God's justice deals in bloody execution. Kingdom is hurly-burly, handy-dandy, winners and losers;[23] might is right, and the bloodier the better. Macbeth takes on what the Thane of Cawdor gives up—the title and the role of usurper (so, for that matter, will Malcolm, at the end; and what about Banquo's posterity: how are *they* going to get possession of the crown?); and it is the king himself who so enthusiastically hands Macbeth his own assassin's knife, like a royal truncheon. My own contribution to a "How Many Children Had Lady Macbeth"

–type essay would be a demonstration that the saintly Duncan *must*, on the circumstantial evidence of these first scenes, not only have usurped the throne himself, but have done it in a particularly foul and gory manner; and that a payoff was made in the bargain. (I am aware that Holinshed provides sources for none of these speculations, except for Macbeth's "crueltie"; but Shakespeare dramatizes and poetizes only what he wants to, and implications and projections from the world of *Macbeth* can be legitimized, if at all, only out of the probabilities established by and in the poetry.)[24]

We need linger only shortly over Macbeth's second meeting with the witches to watch the collaboration of heroic kingly ambition with the powers of darkness at work. King Macbeth uses charms and spells and incantations and staged declarations to assert and nail down his claim to the throne, as had King Duncan; but now the resemblance to demonic methods is open. The witches greet their mistress with "How now, Hecate, you look angerly"; Macbeth (accredited to the wicked as one of them, by the pricking of thumbs) begins, "How now, you secret, black, and midnight hags, What is't you do?" and immediately begins to conjure, using a bloodcurdling litany of destructiveness complementary to the ingredients of the bubbling cauldron. He is rewarded by the apparition of spokesmen for his thought-desires (as the bleeding captain was for Duncan's. This was a prime device of Shakespeare's; look forward, for a moment, to Prospero's staging of the masque of Ceres to "enact" his "present fancies"): an armed head, a bloody child, a child crowned. The first tells him to beware of Macduff, and he finds the caution "good." The bloody one bids him be "bloody, bold, and resolute"; the crowned one, "Be lion-mettled, proud, and take no care who chafes." The witches have said that their charm would be "firm and good," and Hecate commended their pains, "And everyone shall share in the gains." Except for Macbeth's demand for complete satisfaction, which of course backfires (Duncan's blew him up later, by a delayed fuse), the scene is a pretty faithful echo of the first two we have examined. The promise of the prophecy is that *rebellion's* head will not rise successfully against Macbeth. *This* great King, too, may kindly say that the duties of *these* kinsmen repaid their welcome. Blood is good! The gains are worth the pains. "Sweet bodements! good!" The justice of it pleases.

The theme of reporting, tale-telling, begins to sound again in V.iii. Macbeth, defying any more augury as he throws the other kind of physic to the dogs, commands, "Bring me no more reports, let them fly all." His servant and Seyton adumbrate briefly the captain-and-Ross trope of the opening; then, in V.v, following hard upon the potent word-magic of the "Tomorrow and tomorrow and tomorrow" speech with its hammerblow ending,

> it is a tale,
> Told by an idiot, full of sound and fury,
> Signifying nothing,

enters the Messenger. He is now seen to be not only a reporter, but the player of a part—the abstracter and brief chronicler of the time. Malcolm and Duncan had tried to use the captain both after their own honor and dignity and according to his desert: a bloody man, a good and hardy soldier, a brave friend, whose words they accept for as well becoming of him (and them) as his wounds and for smacking of honor (his and theirs). Macbeth's messenger—like his cream-faced-loon-goose-lily-livered-boy-patch-wheyface-servant —is forced to strut and fret, a liar and a slave, an idiot-soothsayer. He is commanded, conjured, to use his tongue, to tell his story, to say it to the king. "Gracious my lord," he begins, attempting to follow the formula, "I should report that which I say I saw, But know not how to do it." He reports the strange event of Birnam Wood beginning to move, and still must speak; he will hang if he speaks false, but "If thy speech be sooth," then this kind of truth lies and re-augurs Macbeth's identity with death. Soothsaying is equivocation, and can be invoked with impunity only by fiends, madmen, and murderers. Duncan could (or thought he could) let the bleeding captain off from his horrendous duty as reporter; this echo by King Macbeth coils back upon saintly King Duncan, and provides a monitory note of prologue to the imperial theme as it is taken up by King-to-be Malcolm in his turn: he has given orders for his soldiers to move Birnam Wood, "and make discovery Err in report of us." Macduff has ratified this and appropriated (once more) the rights and rites of war for the new swelling act:

> Let our just censures
> Attend the true event, and put we on
> Industrious soldiership.

The play ends as it began, and in the same subversively ominous terms—even though the butcher and his fiendlike queen have been expunged from Scotland. Again, there are the reports of battle; Young Siward has displayed his prowess as a man and God's soldier, and has had a fair death. "Hail, King; for so thou art," chants Macduff: "The time is free." The king is again surrounded by the pearls of his noblemen, who, when they have joined in the speaking of the incantatory salutation, "Hail, king of Scotland!" (how can we keep the witches' "All hail, Macbeth, that shall be king hereafter!" from ringing in our ears?), are immediately paid off by being made earls. Malcolm says grace. But surely these pious exhortations cannot be taken at face value, as many readers and critics take them. Not even considering the impact of Malcolm's scene with Macduff in England, or the remark that "gracious England hath Lent us good Siward, Christendom's oldest and best soldier, and ten thousand warlike men, worthy fellows," which is followed by Menteith's statement about the motivation of this holy crusading power, "Revenges burn in them, for their dear causes Would to the bleeding and the grim alarm Excite the mortified man"—even ignoring all this, the last scene is inexorably contaminated by what has gone before. Malcolm's obsession with monetary values and payment—the day has been cheaply bought; young Siward has paid a soldier's debt (paid his score, his father says); sorrow is measured by worth, and Malcolm will spend it, even before he spends an expense of time in reckoning with his followers' loves, getting even with them—is more insistent than was Duncan's, although Malcolm has not as yet, to pay off his ten thousand Christian soldiers, mulcted his enemy of $10,000. Duncan too had declared that the time was free; and this is his son, who has learned only one thing that his father did not know, that Macbeth, however valiant and honorable, was a bloody butcher. The king is dead; long live the king! And here's a bloody usurper's cursed head to prove it. Macduff (whom Malcolm had not long before exchanged misgivings with) is now the worthy gentleman; and we are ready for the cycle to begin again, much as at the inconclusive conclusions of the English history plays.

Irving Ribner, engaged upon the imposing task of representing Kittredge's long dominant version of Shakespeare, has prepared new introductions to the plays "to give some indications of the directions which modern criticism has taken although specific analyses of individual plays are avoided," inasmuch as "many new issues of which Kittredge was not aware have been raised in recent criticism." He reiterates, however, the long-received assertion that

there is no feeling of negation or despair [in *Macbeth*], for Shakespeare shows us a new order being reborn out of the dissolution of the old; Macbeth presents as powerful and all-embracing a vision of evil as has ever been portrayed in literature, but we are reminded always that evil is an unnatural and not a natural condition of humanity.[25]

I suggest that specific analysis, taking into account the word-magic that constitutes the real demonology of tragedy, would find us always reminded that fair is foul and foul is fair.

To Duncan, Macbeth's actions as related by the captain "smack of honour." In varying degrees, all the names and epithets our language gives to the most highly regarded humanistic values— noble, great, glory and glorious, brave and bravery, grace and gracious, good and goods—are subject to double meaning and ironic commentary in Shakespeare; but perhaps *honor—honorable, honest*—comes under his most persistent and telling scrutiny and might serve, in this rapid scanning of some of the "infrastructures" in his plays, as an index to his way with such concepts.[26] With momentary recall of a few keynotes of the topic—Hotspur plucking bright honor from the pale-faced moon, by offering his foes "to the fire-eyed maid of smoky war, All hot and bleeding, so Mars may sit on his altar up to the ears in blood"; Falstaff not liking such grinning honor as Sir Walter Blunt hath; Troilus and Paris persuading Hector that Helen is a theme of honor and renown and that "the soil of her fair rape" can be wiped off in honorable keeping of her; Laertes prating about his "terms of honour" as he prepares his unbated and poison-tipped foil; Othello, an honorable murderer, doing naught in hate, but all in honor—let us pass on to *Coriolanus*, for the value of its obvious parallel to *Macbeth*.

Cominius, the General, reports the warlike acts of Coriolanus to the Senators and the tribunes of the people, to see whether they are consonant with honor; and again the speaking of the litany is stressed: "I shall lack voice. The deeds of Coriolanus Should not be uttered feebly. It is held that valor is the chiefest virtue and Most dignifies the haver." (Is there possibly a sardonic redefinition even here? *Noblesse oblige*, but it is a dignity peculiar to the havers, not the havers-not.) "If it be," continues Cominius—that is, I am asserting and assuming that it is—then Coriolanus is honorable without corrival in the world. And how do we know? Because since he was sixteen he has been the bloodiest killer in the Roman army. He drove the bristled lips before; he struck Tarquin to his knees; he waxed like a sea; he lurched all swords of the garland; he made the coward turn terror into sport; men fell before his stem as weeds before a vessel under sail. "His sword, death's stamp, Where it did mark, it took. From face to foot He was a thing of blood"; he struck Corioli like a planet. "He did run reeking o'er the lives of men as if 'Twere perpetual spoil." "Now all's his." Menenius and the Senators, responders to this rite, cry: "Worthy man!" "He's right noble." "He cannot but with measure fit the honors Which we devise him." Much of the rest of this play is an overt and/or subvert critique of the concept of honor in its myriad ramifications; but this complacent glorying in bloodthirstiness as the soul of "deed-achieving honor," by a professional soldier and self-seeking patricians, stands as one of the set pieces of the play, defining Coriolanus. It has usually been read with as straight a face as has the report of *Macbeth's* bloody captain.

Coriolanus is certainly one of Shakespeare's Roman plays, if it does not fit the usual requirements of tragedy;[27] and it has been recognized for some time that the concept of Romanism was one of the leading sources of Tudor self-congratulation. After all, Britain was founded by Brut, descendant of Aeneas, was it not? British virtues were Roman virtues. Even Horatio, that paragon of the phlegmatic Englishman, would like to think of himself as more of an antique Roman than a Dane; Macbeth refuses to play the Roman fool and die on his own sword only when he has renounced his Scottish allegiance and become a hound of hell. The Augustan Peace reached England in Cymbeline's time, with a Roman and a British ensign waving together. Not only are there Senators, with Latin names, in Timon's Athens, but the gods who oversee these Greeks are Mars and Diana, Hymen and Plutus; and in *Theseus's* Athens Cupid and Venus (not Eros and Aphrodite) operate through those very British divinities, Oberon, Titania, Peaseblossom, and Robin Goodfellow. Even on the plains of Troy itself, the master mind of traditional Greek treacherousness is Ulysses, not Odysseus. And so on. Shakespeare reflected, as always, *on the surface* of his Roman plays the incredible mixture of jingoism and complacent anachronism (to be seen at large, for example, in *The Faerie Queene*) which is the mystique of Briticism. But the play that undertakes to examine the mystique of Romanism itself, with its cult of honor and nobility, is of course *Julius Caesar;* and it is primarily about Brutus, not Caesar, for this was the noblest Roman of them all.

If we can take Sisson's suggestion that the action of the first part of *Macbeth* is the winning of Macbeth for Duncan and his group,[28] *Julius Caesar* also might find its theme in Cinna's remark to Cassius, "if you could But win the noble Brutus to our party." They win him all right, nobleness and all, to find that, like Duncan, they have caught a tartar. Ligarius is miraculously cured, "By all the gods that Romans bow before," if Brutus, "Soul of Rome, Brave son, derived from honorable loins!" "have in hand Any exploit worthy the name of honor." (I have reversed the chronology, but an eerie echoing cross-reference to *Macbeth* follows immediately: "Thou [Brutus], like an exorcist, hast conjured up My mortified spirit"—remember Menteith's use of this unusual trope.) "What's to do? (Brutus): A piece of work that will make sick men whole. (Ligarius, leering in anticipation): But are not some whole that we must make sick? (Brutus): That must we also." For Brutus is an honorable man, sacrificing not butchering his enemy in the high Roman fashion. He has reasons full of good regard for slaughtering Caesar. He is "contented Caesar shall Have all true rites and lawfull ceremonies"— and the sly spirit ironical adds, "It shall advantage more than do us wrong."[29]

In school I had to learn and recite with conviction not only Polonius's advice to Laertes but also Antony's curtain-eulogy of Brutus. Even today college as well as high school students in their tens of thousands are taught to swell with pride as they intone the praise of the noblest Roman of them all, with Nature standing up and saying to all the world, "This was a man." These are the official remarks of Roman Antony himself, who damns his own nephew with a spot to momentarily appease Lepidus, a slight unmeritable man, not fit for great things, and who has called (in a soliloquy) upon Ate come hot from hell to revenge Caesar, "The ruins of the noblest man That ever lived in the tide of times" *upon* that very honorable Roman and universal butcher, Brutus. "According to his virtue let us use him," responds Octavius, "Most like a soldier, ordered honorably." But we will know from *Antony and Cleopatra* what Octavius means by the honorable use of Roman virtue; and we again remember that Hamlet, who sardonically advises Polonius to use the players not according to their desert but after his own honor and dignity lest his reputation suffer after his death, knows that it was a brute part of this noblest Roman to have killed so capital a calf in the Capitol of Rome. *Julius Caesar* is so much under the sway of the savagely critical demon—more so than even *Troilus and Cressida* or *Coriolanus*—that here the Spirit Ironical has been hoist with his own petar. Not content with even such observations as Cassius's "Well, Brutus, thou art noble, Yet I see thy honorable mettle may be wrought From that it is disposed" or the unmistakable evidence of Brutus's stuffed-shirted self-righteousness,[30] the play comes out boldly and lashes every one of these capital crooks with *noble, honorable, great, wise, valiant, honor, noble, noble, Roman, noble, noble,* until one would think it impossible not to see what is going on; but here Shakespeare has overreached himself and suffered the fate of the critic who finds his most extravagant ironies taken at face value. He was more careful, and more subtle, when he returned to the attack in *Macbeth* and *Antony and Cleopatra*—although even there, when he has Pompey bearding Octavius and Antony, the snarling words come pouring out:

> What was't
> That mov'd pale Cassius to conspire, and what
> Made the all-honored honest Roman, Brutus,
> With the armed rest, courtiers of beauteous freedom,
> To drench the Capitol. . . .

But in 1598–99, while this strong upsurge of the tragic troll was in possession of him, he also wrote *King Henry V*. Will it be too outrageous to find therein a critique of Briticism, to match that of Romanism?

Dean Frye, examining the question of Shakespearean parody, finds to his disgruntlement that "critical attempts to turn *Henry V* into *Troilus and Cressida* should amaze no one; there is still a growing tendency to read most of Shakespeare in this way."[31] At the risk of ending up on the side of the horned angels, I would like to welcome this tendency, and look at *Henry V* briefly for a prime demonstration of Shakespearean history as a critique of humanism under the aegis of aggressive patriotism. Its theme, I suggest, is What price glory?

Note first the unusual presence of the choruses, one for each act, and their insistent reminder of the need for the services of the imagination, defying the requirements of both time and place, if the impact of this reenactment is to be grasped:

Oh, pardon! Since a crooked figure may Attest in little place a million, And let us, ciphers to this great accompt, On your imaginary forces work. . . . Piece out our imperfections with your thoughts. . . . Play with your fancies. . . . Follow, follow. Grapple your minds to sternage of this navy. . . . Work, work your thoughts, and therein see a siege. Behold the ordnance . . . with fatal mouths gaping on girded Harfleur. . . . And the nimble gunner . . . now the devilish cannon touches And down goes all before them. Still be kind, And eke out our performance with your mind. . . . Now entertain conjecture of a time When creeping murmur and the poring dark Fills the wide vessel of the universe . . . through the foul womb of night. . . . The country cocks do crow, the clocks do toll, And the third hour of drowsy morning name. . . . Yet sit and see, Minding true things by what their mockeries be. . . . Now behold, In the quick forge and working-house of thought, How London doth pour out her citizens! The mayor and all his brothers in best sort, Like to the Senators of antique Rome With the plebeians swarming at their heels, Go forth and fetch their conquering Caesar in. As, by a lower but loving likelihood, Were now the General of our gracious Empress . . . from Ireland coming, Bringing rebellion broached on his sword. . . .

An incredible audacity of Shakespeare's, urging his auditory to open Pandora's box and let out that Ariel to whom thought is free to find the truth behind the mockeries of patriotism, that last refuge of scoundrels. The ideal bringing into being, under the aegis of foreign aggrandizement, of what might be called Great Britain or the United Kingdom (King, clergy, nobles, common people; representative warriors from Scotland, Ireland, Wales as well as England) has already been fatally contaminated by our knowledge of Henry IV's advice to his son that his course is to busy giddy English minds with foreign quarrels so that they will not be tempted to look too nearly into his title to the crown. To be sure, Henry came back victorious (but alas, not so did Essex), a conquering hero; but by this treatment Shakespeare only proves, I think, the vitality and tenacity of his oppositional and deviationist spirit, in that it does so subtly undermine and take the gloss off so officially glorious a victory as Agincourt.[32]

Luckily, most of this exegesis has been done already,[33] and I can merely reiterate the elaborate and venal casuistry whereby the Archbishop and Bishop send the eagle England in prey with God's blessing; or the fulsome self-righteousness of Henry as he lectures the conspirators about treachery as *the* original sin, before he announces "every rub is smoothed on our way. Then forth, dear countrymen, . . . the signs of our advance, No King of England if not King of France" (echoes of Richard II, as he shoved Gaunt into his grave and forfeited his estates: "So much for that. Now for these Irish wars!"). Or the antiphon, in the very next scene, by that band of brothers, Henry's former companions Nym, Bardolph, and Pistol: "Yokefellows in arms, Let us to France, like horse-leeches, my boys. To suck, to suck, the very blood to suck." Or Henry's "But if it be a sin to covet honor, I am the most offending soul alive." (It is, and he is, remarks the small voice, under the booming rhetoric. And Henry knew it, when, as Crown Prince, he parodied Hotspur, his "factor.") Or the little touch of Harry in the night, calling his soldiers brothers, friends, countrymen (Friends, Romans, countrymen, says Antony, lend me your ears), trying as far as his aristocratic fastidiousness will let him to "distill observingly some soul of goodness in things evil," "gather honey from the weed," and "make a moral of the Devil himself"; but he doesn't succeed very well, for, as Williams points out, how can warriors charitably dispose of anything when blood is their argument?

The play may be seen as a study in what it means to be a soldier-king. And Henry, even as he prays to the God of Battles and hastily hands over his victory to God for justification (with the death penalty for anybody who lays claim to any of the praise for it), cannot keep the baleful words from coming out, in the horrendously Tammerlane-like (or Agamemnon-like) ultimatum to the defenders of Harfleur: "What is it to me if imperious war, Arrayed in flames like the Prince of Fiends, Do, with his smirched complexion, all fell feats Enlinked to waste and desolation? . . . What rein can hold licentious wickedness When down the hill he holds his fierce career?" If they, guilty in defense, don't surrender unconditionally, they must in a moment look to see the blind and bloody soldier give his control over to "the filthy and contagious clouds of heady murder, spoil, and villainy." This, just after he has sworn "As I am a soldier—A name that in my thoughts becomes me best." The French marauders "burned and carried away all that was in the King's tent, wherefore the King, most worthily, hath caused every soldier to cut his prisoner's throat. Oh," agree Gower and Fluellen, those professors of the excellent discipline of arms, " 'tis a gallant King." ("It is a peerless kinsman," said Duncan.) "Take me," says Harry the bluff wooer to Katherine of France, "take a soldier. Take a soldier, take a king." He had spent his early life preparing to be England's king *par excellence*, taking various ingredients in the mixture from his father, his brother John, Hotspur—and Falstaff, from whom he also learned that " 'tis no sin for a man to labor in his vocation." "When thou art King . . . let men say that we be men of good government, being governed . . . by our noble and chaste mistress the moon, under whose countenance we steal." Although Prince Henry examines this bit of *force majeure* casuistry, with quips and quiddities, even up to the ridge of the gallows, he has absorbed its ethic; Majesty, with or without Grace, prevails.

"Nice customs," as well in the diplomatic wooing chamber as on the field of warlike arbitrament, "courtesy to great Kings. . . . We are the makers of manners . . . and the liberty that follows our places stops the mouth of all find-faults." Mouths can be stopped by cutting throats as well as by kissing lips.

All the spokesmen in the play have something to say about this built-in evil of war as the instrument of policy and an attribute of kings,[34] including the voice of "treacherous" France, Burgundy— and it casts its sombre shadow over every ringing hosannah to English greatness and honor. I do not remember that Churchill, in England's finest hour, quoted much more than "Once more into the breach, dear friends, once more, Or else close the wall up with our English dead"—but the horrendous underpinnings of honor come pouring out of Henry's mouth, in unstoppable self-incrimination, in the play's body:

> In peace there's nothing so becomes a man
> As modest stillness and humility.
> But when the blast of war blows in our ears,
> Then imitate the action of the tiger,
> . . .
> Disguise fair nature with hard-favored rage.
> . . .   Let the brow o'erwhelm it
> As fearfully as doth a galled rock
> O'erhang and jutty his confounded base,
> Swilled with the wild and wasteful ocean.
> . . .   On, on, you noblest English,
> Whose blood is fet from fathers of war proof!
> . . .
> Dishonor not your mothers . . .
> Be copy now to men of grosser blood,
> And teach them how to war . . .
> Follow your spirit, and upon this charge,
> Cry "God for Harry, England, and Saint George!"

And perforce, for the Prince of Fiends. (One might say, out of Henry's own mouth, that the royal English motto should rather be *Diable et mon Droit*.) If we have indeed taken the sparks that come flying from the quick forge and working-house of thought, there is no warrant for even the chastened and dubious hope at the end, "*May* our oaths well-kept and prosperous be," or need for the epilogue that reminds us that this glorious episode of the Star of England was only—and inevitably—the prelude to the Wars of the Roses, "that made his England bleed—which oft our stage hath shown." It hath shown it too even here, presented in the crooked figures and ciphers of tragic poetry.[35]

These few indices of Shakespeare's underlying tragic sense as a critique of humanism, and its pretensions, from the inside, will have to suffice here, although they can be ramified almost indefinitely, down into the most joyful of the comedies. I should like to spend the remainder of this chapter on evidences of his preoccupation, even obsession, with the overplot of tragedy, with what Harry Levin has identified in Shakespeare as "an indication that the play at hand is but an interlude from a universal drama performed in the great *theatrum mundi*."[36] The hard core of this is, What about the gods? Are they benevolent as well as omnipotent? Are they just? And can men stand to share in their justness? Can nonviolent grace be conjured from the gods who sit in grandeur? Shakespeare's great heart kept hoping it might be so; his deep-seeing eye, and his piety to the hard tragic vision, kept saying: I doubt it.[37]

"As flies to wanton boys are we to the gods," says Gloucester, "They kill us for their sport." No difficulty grasping the antinomy here: we, they; them against us; it is the first part of Hardy's "Hap":

> some vengeful god, would call to me
> From up the sky, and laugh, "Thou suffering thing,
> Know that thy sorrow is my ecstasy,
> That thy love's loss is my hate's profiting."

It is the opposite of Dante's comic "In la sua voluntade è nostra pace"; it is hard-core tragedy. But, we are tempted to say with Edgar, this is Gloucester "in ill thoughts" which can be rectified;

and it is an offhand remark by a subplot character, which we mustn't attribute to the author, and it is only the beginning of the fourth act, and so on. But then, *after* Cordelia has come back, with talk about "blest secrets" and "virtues of the earth," "aidant and remediate" to a "good man's distress," Edgar tries some white magic of his own to relieve Gloucester and exorcise the fiend who was tormenting him to despair. And he succeeds, with this admonition,

> It was some fiend, therefore, thou happy father,
> Think that the clearest gods, who make them honors
> Of men's impossibilities, have preserved thee.

Lionel Abel would perhaps read this also as a contradiction of the former saying, like "The gods are just." But if we look at the form and listen with the inner ear, there is something intrusive and subversive going on. Why that qualifying clause, with its reminder that there is a vast discrepancy between the clearest gods and men? Impossibilities for men are honors for *them*; Gloucester's preservation is engineered not for his benefit, but to display the gods' powers. And there is no indication that this is not just as capricious, as wanton, as killing men for their sport.[38]

Again, if we are still hankering, we suppress the insinuation and pass rapidly over Gloucester's rather unecstatic acceptance of his preservation as one in which to "bear affliction till it do cry out itself, 'Enough, enough,' and die," to Edgar's gratuitous assumption that his "patient thoughts" will also be "free"—that is, like those of the clearest gods. But the daemon inside Shakespeare will not leave it there either. In the middle of Lear's instruction of Cordelia in the right and proper way to live for those who take upon them the mystery of things and act as God's spies, the insistent little tune comes in again:

> Upon such sacrifices, my Cordelia,
> The gods themselves throw incense. Have I caught thee?
> He that parts us shall bring a brand from Heaven,
> And fire us hence like foxes.

There are the gods again, acting in ways proper and characteristic and definitive: must we not, if we take the internal connections of poetry seriously, read *themselves* as a reflexive as well as an intensive?[39] The phrase had insinuated itself into Shakespeare's budget of iterative tropes earlier, in the player's speech in *Hamlet:*

> Out, out, thou strumpet Fortune! All you gods,
> In general synod take away her power,
> Break all the spokes and fellies from her wheel,
> And bowl the round nave down the hill of Heaven
> As low as to the fiends! . . .
> Who this had seen, with tongue in venom steeped
> 'Gainst Fortune's state would treason have pronounced,
> But if the gods themselves did see her then,
> When she saw Pyrrhus make malicious sport
> In mincing with his sword her husband's limbs,
> The instant burst of clamor that she made,
> Unless things mortal move them not at all,
> Would have made milch the burning eyes of Heaven
> And passion in the gods. . . .

As Harry Levin points out, the prospect of the gods' feeling an emotional response is stated only conditionally, and "'we are left confronting a dizzying hierarchy of externalized emotion, which continues to refer our query upwards until it is out of sight.'"[40] And at least the seed of implication is there that the important ingredient in the gods' "venomous" passion is self-righteous outrage at *lèse-majesté*, the treason of one of *them* who, having brought dishonor on the whole synod, deserves to be disenfranchised and violently exiled to the nether *spirit*-world. Things mortal might possibly trigger off passion in the gods themselves, but I do not find warrant in the speech for Levin's "characterizing their attitude as compassion, *a* sympathetic participation in the feelings of Hecuba." *Their* catharsis will be achieved (and, presumably, Olympian equanimity restored) by the purging of Fortune's sullied wheel from high heaven straight to hell, bypassing earth and its mortal concerns. What's Hecuba to them? Gods do not throw incense on a sacrifice for the benefit of the sacrificer or the victim, but for themselves. As even Albany blurts out, "This judgment of the heavens, that makes us tremble, Touches us not with pity." And his appeal, "The gods defend her," is answered mutely by the sight of Cordelia dead in Lear's arms; for all Lear's assumption of godly honors, he found her defense an impossibility and could only kill the slave that was a-hanging her. "Is this the promis'd end?" asks Albany, meaning both Is *this* what we have been led to hope for, our salvation? and This is pretty close, in its imaging of horror, to the threatened day of doom. "Fall and cease."

I trust that we may still place *King Lear* among the tragedies of the Shakespeare canon, in spite of those who would turn its apocalypse into an alleluia.[41] One means to this worthy end is to follow the internal corroboration that most of the rest of the canon, in its comedy-tragedy spectrum, provides. *Timon of Athens* is close to *Lear* and may well have been a kind of pendant to it (and *Coriolanus*), whereby Shakespeare seems to be giving free rein to the Spirit Ironical, perhaps in a desperate attempt to exorcise it by bringing it out into the open; and it cross-references this particular tragic core for us nicely. Timon, who presumes to be godlike in philanthropy, finds that it produces its very opposite. It drives *him* to madness and desperation, but leaves Flavius, the good-hearted faithful servant, bewildered and cast down: "Strange, unusual blood," he says, "When man's worst sin is he does too much good! Who then dares be half so kind again? For bounty, that makes gods, does still mar men." Timon indicts the gods in his curse on gold, the "sweet king-killer," "bright defiler": "thou visible god, That solder'st close impossibilities And makest them kiss!" And he leaves Athens and its senators "To the protection of the prosperous gods, As thieves to keepers." This version of Shakespeare's exploration of man's life as an affair with the gods is certainly a Blasphemy as well as a Misanthropy.

He had tried previously (probably before *Lear*) to enforce (even with capital letters) the opposite assertion, in *All's Well*

That Ends Well. Helena, to achieve her own vision of good even at the risk of her life, boldly takes upon herself the mystery of things: she can "cure the desperate languishings whereof the King is rendered lost"; she swears "by grace itself"; she urges the King to "make an experiment of Heaven," to challenge the gods to make their honors available to resolve men's impossibilities. "He that of greatest works is finisher Oft does them by the weakest minister." (Wheels within wheels! Here is a minister of heaven who claims she needn't be a scourge. And the god is invoked under his aspect of completer, Zeus Teleios, whom Clytemnestra called upon to "accomplish these my prayers"—Clytemnestra the sister of Helen, the Destroyer; and Shakespeare called his man-trapping heroine Helena, though it was Giletta in the source.) The good Countess prays God's blessing into Helena's attempt, and ratifies her assertion that her doctor-father's "good receipts Shall for my legacy be sanctified By the luckiest stars in Heaven." The king is persuaded: "Methinks in thee some blessed spirit doth speak His powerful sound within an organ weak; And what impossibility would slay In common sense, sense saves another way." And of course it works; the King is made well.

But for all this enforcement (and it is hammered home in rhyming couplets too), not only does the play as a whole leave a bad taste in the mouth—the King says at the end, dubiously, "All yet *seems* well"—but also the critic-censor is sniping away at the assertion even while it is triumphant. "Little Helen" has told us in a soliloquy that her real motive and her real faith are not quite so pious:

> Our remedies oft in ourselves do lie,
> Which we ascribe to Heaven.   The fatal sky
> Gives us free scope.   Only doth backward pull
> Our slow designs when we ourselves are dull.
> What power is it which mounts my love so high,
> That makes me see, and cannot feed mine eye
> . . .

Impossible be strange attempts to those
That weigh their pains in sense and do suppose
What hath not been cannot be.

(Iago and Edmund say much the same thing.) Lafeu, the half-cynical commentator of the play, takes the gloss off the cure itself and its easy assumption as proof of the beneficence of heaven by engaging in a mocking duet with Parolles: he does precisely the same as Hamlet parodying Osric, in putting the reiteration of "the very hand of Heaven," "a showing of a heavenly effect in an earthly actor," into the crooked mouth of Parolles, the corrupter of words, of whom it is said, "Is it possible he should know what he is, and be that he is?" And it is here that the independent spirit of tragedy finds its spokesman, in Lafeu's cryptic, riddling, prose introduction:

> They say miracles are past, and we have our philosophical persons, to make modern and familiar things supernatural and causeless. Hence it is that we make trifles of terrors, ensconcing ourselves into seeming knowledge when we should submit ourselves to an unknown fear.

Like the other problem plays, tragi-comedies, of this uneasy period of Shakespeare, *All's Well* resorts to tricks to achieve its kingly humanistic ends—and finds that the gods are past masters at trickery, which is only a euphemistic form of treachery.[42]

But Shakespeare, unlike most of his Jacobean contemporaries in tragedy and unlike Kafka, who found his world of words undergoing a hideous disintegration,[43] was able to find new holds for wrestling with his demon or, rather, new ways of slipping momentarily free of the hammerlock of that Mephistophelean adversary, the spirit of negation. It is my belief that *Antony and Cleopatra* was his breakthrough, from another stance. He does not, to my apprehension, raise the question of *l'affaire dieux* much in this play;[44] but Cleopatra (for whom "vilest things Become themselves in her, that the holy priests Bless her when she is riggish," who "makes defect perfection And, breathless, power breathes forth," and Antony ("heavenly mingle," whom "the very violence of his sadness or merriment becomes So does it no man else") assume godliness in their espousal of the principle of fluidity—infinite virtue in infinite variety. (*Infinite* belongs to Antony and Cleopatra, while *absolute* is resigned to Caesar and Pompey. Caesar is the "universal landlord"; Antony is "infinite virtue." It is the difference between worldly and godlike majesty.) Eternity was in their lips and eyes, none of their parts so poor but was a race of heaven. It would become proper, when Antony was dead, for Cleopatra to throw her scepter at the injurious gods and tell them that this world did equal theirs until they had stolen her jewel.

Antony and Cleopatra are both riggish, botchers ever, and as unethical as the gods themselves;[45] and they beguile Caesar. "Think you there was, or might be," asks Cleopatra, "such a man As this I dreamed of?" To Dolabella's Roman No, she counters imperiously, "You lie, up to the hearing of the gods," who alone, along with the poet (their spokesman and minister), can make honors out of men's impossibilities. "Nature wants stuff To vie strange forms with fancy, yet to imagine An Antony were nature's piece 'gainst fancy, Condemning shadows quite." The play is Shakespeare's study in the dynamics of disintegration, where the dream of a transcendent embrace, confronted by the fact of defeat in the form of continual slippings and partings, achieves its more-than-acquiescence in melting, discandying, dissolving, untying, of the knots intrinsicate: this time the dream is accomplished in the mysterious godlike way, through the fact.[46] It is not all triumph, by any means—the critical spirit is operating here too and gives some telling blows—but it *does* penetrate up to the hearing of the gods and it opens the way out of the tragic gods-men impasse to the sea-changes of *Pericles* and *Cymbeline* and *The Winter's Tale* and *The Tempest*.

Whatever we think of *Pericles* and *Cymbeline* as artistic successes or failures, they are full of testimony to Shakespeare's preoccupation with our tragic trope and with the fearsome and never quite confidently grasped godlike power of the poet. Pericles begins his princely pilgrimage with a riddling ordeal involving the tragic knowledge that the perfections of the gods are deadly to men and that "Kings are earth's gods; in vice their law's their will; And if Jove stray, who dares say Jove doth ill?" And, further, the freedom of the whole is the destiny of the part: Pericles's coming to *know* the secrets of such personages is his death warrant, "Therefore instantly this prince must die, For by his fall my honor must keep high." There is some wishful theorizing, as "Princes in this should live like gods above, Who freely give to every one that comes To honor them," and "the most high gods' " meting out vengeful justice upon the incestuous Antiochus and his daughter. But we have already seen what cold comfort there is in a justice based on vengeance. The old tune soon comes back: "O you gods! Why do you make us love your goodly gifts, And snatch them straight away? We here below Recall not what we give, and therein may Use honour with you."

But, as everyone knows, *Pericles* is a diptych; and with the birth of Marina the gods take on a new look. The marvelous brothel scenes—in which Marina, calling upon the clear gods to set her free from unhallowedness, undoes an unholy profession by freezing the god Priapus—show the vulnerability of tragic formulas to being conjured inside out. "How now?" cries the bawd, "What's the matter?" "Worse and worse, mistress. She has here spoken holy words to the Lord Lysimachus." "Oh, abominable!" "She makes our profession as it were to stink afore the face of the gods." Macbeth, the witches, and Hecate in reverse! Pompey Bum's trade, and Mistress Quickly's, invulnerable to the whipping of old father antic the law, dissolves into its proper putrefaction at the potent breath of a pure votaress. Unlike Helena, Marina cures her king without challenging the heavens, but with their full blessing; she is godlike perfect without being malignant. Pericles can reverse the usual formula: "Thank the holy gods as loud As thunder threatens us." Lord Cerimon, "through whom the gods have shown their power," is a reverend sir, and "the gods can have no mortal officer

More like a god" than he. Shakespeare's tragic, selfish gods have, in this post-tragic play, gone the way of the Eumenides. Still, Gower (the presenter of this parable and the rather anxious proponent of the imagination as the means of accomplishing its miracle) has the last word; and his announcement of the triumph of "virtue, led on by heaven," and of truth, faith, loyalty, and learned charity is preceded and followed by a reaffirmation of the negative *sine qua non:* Monstrous lust has had its due and just reward; "The gods for murder seemed so content To punish, although not done but meant." (Even in *Measure for Measure,* this vindictiveness is lacking.) *Their* honors, first and last, must be preserved; their justice takes precedence over charity.

Cymbeline marches to its Augustan Peace to a steady tune of piety and willed imprecation: prayer is as much a charm and a formula as cursing. Imogen, "more goddesslike than wifelike," exemplar of the chameleon-poet's perfectly good source of delight for Keats, is pious and (ultimately) potent. She calls: "You good gods, Let what is here contained relish of love, Of my lord's health, of his content. . . . Good news, gods!" Earlier she says her nightly prayers, "To your protection I commend me, gods! From fairies and the tempters of the night Guard me, beseech ye." The pastoral genius Belarius and his two princely changelings apparently know, like Adam and Eve before the fall, "how to adore the Heavens" and to bow "to a morning's holy office": "Hail, thou fair Heaven!" Prince Arviragus officially goes along with Providence: "Let ordinance come as the gods foresay it." Posthumus, when he returns to Britain from his truancy, takes up his part of the antiphon: "Do your best wills, And make me blest to obey!" Cymbeline himself ranges by his side his earthly saviors, compassed with *his* kingdom's pearl: "You whom the gods have made Preservers of my throne"— gods had this time made honors for men, not themselves. Unlike Lear with Cordelia (or Gloucester, whose heart, though smilingly, burst), Cymbeline reacts safely to Imogen's only apparent death with an expanded reverse oxymoron: "If this be so, the gods do mean to strike me To death with mortal joy." The soothsayer— now an intermediary between gods' knowledge and men's—asserts at the end an epiphany: "The fingers of the powers above do tune The harmony of this peace" (*In la sua voluntade è nostra pace*). And the king wraps it up, most strikingly apropos to our purpose, with the old incense image from *Lear* now purified and hallowed: "Laud we the gods, And let our crooked smokes climb to their nostrils From our blest altars." Even crooked! The gods may be devious in their ways and write straight with crooked lines; but now man throws the incense on, confident that his smoke will corkscrew its way to the heavens and find itself not poisonous of that clear atmosphere. It is a sustained counterattack on the demon of imprecation, twisting his arm with his own holds and exerting a new-found brute strength into the bargain.

To be sure, the adversary has been fighting, or at least refusing to knuckle under, all along. The episode in Imogen's bedroom (with its mysterious and ominous setting, doubtless the prototype, along with Cleopatra's barge, of the opening scene in the Game of Chess section of *The Waste Land*) is *Lear*-like in menace and apparent callousness: Imogen prays for protection against tempters of the night, and forthwith Iachimo comes from the trunk. When he has done his dirty work, he entombs himself again with "I lodge in fear. Though this a heavenly angel, Hell is here." Arviragus qualifies his acquiescence in the ordinance of the gods with "Howsoever, My brother hath done well" to kill Cloten. Posthumus, hard upon his declaration of obedience, declines to do what he was brought by the gods to Britain for and substitutes his will for theirs: "Therefore, good Heavens, Hear patiently *my* purpose." Cymbeline, like Pericles, cannot begin his peace until he has announced (and sanctioned) the merciless retribution visited upon his "wicked Queen; Whom Heavens in justice both on her and hers Have laid most heavy hand." Shakespeare, it seems to me, is striking back in this play with a rather heavy hand himself—the best evidence of which is that *tour de force*, the apparition scene, in which the ghosts of Posthumus's family, the Leonati, call Jupiter down to face their charges of godly injustice and frivolity:

> Sicilius. No more, thou thunder master, show
>   Thy spite on mortal flies.
> With Mars fall out, with Juno chide,
>   That thy adulteries
>   Rates and revenges.
>   . . .
>
> I. Bro. Then, Jupiter, thou King of gods,
>   Why hast thou thus adjourned
> The graces for his merits due,
>   Being to all dolors turned?
> Thy crystal windows ope. Look out.
>   No longer exercise
> Upon a valiant race thy harsh
>   And potent injuries.
> Mother. Since, Jupiter, our son is good,
>   Take off his miseries,
> Peep through thy marble mansion, help,
>   Or we poor ghosts will cry
> To the shining synod of the rest
>   Against thy deity.
> Both Bros. Help, Jupiter, or we appeal,
>   And from thy justice fly.

This is, surely, a willfully comic and audacious parody of *Job*. (I would go Kitto one better and say that Shakespeare is never so dangerous as when he is writing doggerel.) Jupiter descends in thunder, riding on an eagle, and harangues the protesters back with "Hush! How dare you? . . . No farther with your din Express impatience, lest you stir up mine"—and off he goes back to his radiant roof. His "celestial breath was sulphurous to smell"—the gods themselves throwing incense. But unlike the riddling browbeating of the Voice from the Whirlwind, Jupiter has explained somewhat how Providence works:

Jup. Be not with mortal accidents opprest,
       No care of yours it is. You know 'tis ours.
       Whom best I love I cross, to make my gift,
       The more delayed, delighted. Be content.

Posthumus will be "happier much by his affliction made." Sweet
are the uses of the adversatives of the gods. And all the ghosts, before going off to gain blessedness by performing his will, cry,
"Thanks, Jupiter!" It is very difficult not (and perhaps not altogether illegitimate) to import modern slang intonations into this
egregious piece of Gilbertian doggerel-parody; at any rate, reading
it thus, as part of Shakespeare's campaign to trick the Spirit Ironical
with sleight of hand, is better, I submit, than Johnson's ponderous
umbrage, that to pay any attention to it "were to waste criticism
upon unresisting imbecility."[47]

The Winter's Tale and of course The Tempest have been expli-
cated more than sufficiently, as Shakespeare's final triumph over his
tragic vision, his emergence onto the plateau of joy and serenity, of
having found out not only a new earth, a brave new world, but new
and gracious heavens too. We all know how The Winter's Tale,
like Alcestis and The Cocktail Party, turn things dying or dead to
things newborn. "This is fairy gold, boy, and 'twill prove so."
"Nothing but Bonfires." I would like merely to draw upon this
general apprehension and understanding of the play to corroborate
the continuing relevance and centrality of our tragic tropes; if they
are found here, transfigured and turned inside out, then we can be
reasonably confident that they were all along the touchstones of
Shakespeare's hard tragic sense. And sure enough, they turn up, in
dozens of variations. Think only of the report of Dion and Cleomenes about the oracle, with its praise of the delicate climate and
sweet air (not sulphurous), the ceremonious and unearthly sacrifice; "But of all, the burst And the ear-deafening voice of th'oracle,
Kin of Jove's thunder, so surprised" their senses that they were
nothing, yet, their journey was to them rare and pleasant. And
think especially of our figure, "the gods themselves." Autolycus,

trying desperately to be constant to his profession of thief and cozener, is prevented: "Sure the gods do this year connive at us, and we may do anything extempore." "If I had a mind to be honest, I see Fortune would not suffer me. She drops booties in my mouth." Timon's *either/or* has given way to *both/and*, the unearned increment, the bonus: "I am courted now with a double occasion, gold *and* a means to do the Prince my master good." *Besides* other good reasons for doing things her way, says Paulina, "the gods Will have fulfilled their secret purposes." Cleomenes, only a little prematurely, can counsel the King to "At the last, Do as the Heavens have done, Forget your evil, With them forgive yourself."

But of course the best spokesman for this by now decontaminated and de-fused insight is Florizel, justifying to Perdita pranking her up as Flora, most goddess-like—Perdita, fresh piece of excellent witchcraft, all of whose acts are queens. This is a play of *felix culpa* and *sursum corda;* and Florizel enounces all the themes together: "Lift up your countenance. . . . Apprehend nothing but jollity. The gods themselves, Humbling their deities to love, have taken The shapes of beasts upon them. . . . Their transformations were never for a piece of beauty rarer." The sheep-shearing feast "is as a meeting of the petty gods"; and this must mean not the minor gods but that *all* gods are tamed to man's jolly good purposes, for "Jupiter became a bull, and bellowed; the green Neptune A ram, and bleated"—and even Fortune, though "visible an enemy, . . . power no jot Hath . . . to change our loves." The play ends with the full-scale successful *ololugmos:* "You gods, look down And from your sacred vials pour graces Upon my daughter's head." They do not reserve them for themselves, nor do they lose any honor in the process. And, as a special bonus for our own labors, this play of plenitude gives us another whitewashed tragic demon, whom we met before with the tag, For every winner there must be at least one loser. Many times earlier, Shakespeare has presented this sticky burr, notably even in the comedies and histories, as well as in the problem plays and tragedies; but here Paulina, that miracle-working old turtle, dismisses the company with "Go together, you precious winners all." No losers! Not even Leontes, once as thrall to jealousy and a divinity of hell as Othello; not even the gods, who, blessed and blessing, are still themselves.

To interpret *The Tempest* has been difficult (it so full of dazzling sideshows, subplots, and overplots), but I now think the action of the play can be described as having to do with Prospero's attempt to achieve true detachment through successful art, and through the achievement of renunciation (relinquishment, quietus) of godlike honors without destroying or corrupting himself and others in the process. Prospero, and consequently Shakespeare himself, may ultimately emerge for our time as the crucial hero of the canon on the score of critical-versus-romantic.

The romantic view takes Prospero at face value as supreme, in charge, the kindly-disposed providential magician-priest who brings into being a brave new world—nothing but bonfires again. And, sure enough, near the end old Gonzalo sounds the last refrain of our curse-turned-benediction: "Look down, you gods, And on this couple drop a blessed crown! For it is you that have chalked forth the way Which brought us hither." And both Alonzo and Gonzalo enunciate the word of joyful acquiescence: "Be it so!"— that Amen which stuck in Macbeth's throat and came only querulously perverted from Edgar and Albany ("Is this the promised end? Or image of that horror?"). Even Caliban, thing of darkness and demidevil (unlike that other demidevil Iago, who would be demanded nothing), says "Aye" and will seek for grace. But again, and definitively, we are given an agon, a struggle both with and against that wrestling angel with horns who must be come to terms with in the time available: "I find," says Prospero, "My zenith doth depend upon a most auspicious star, whose influence If now I court not, but omit, my fortunes Will ever after droop." And it is an anxious, passionate, mind-beating process. Prospero's is a rough magic, rough with the destructive potency of the gods: "To the dread rattling thunder Have I given fire, and rifted Jove's stout oak with his own bolt." (Remember Othello's occupation.) He has succeeded, by his Jovian usurpation of the isle and Caliban's heritage, only in teaching Caliban to curse; and he can call Caliban only by cursing, himself. He is testy and jittery when trying to exorcise, by reenactment and drawing Miranda back into the dark backward and abysm of time. He scolds and blasts Ariel in the same terms as he uses for Caliban, as a "malignant thing"—Ariel who is the very spirit of freedom, longing for autonomy, but who, after all, was the servant of the damned witch Sycorax, who could peg this genie into a gnarled oak, but could not let him out again. *Odi et amo;* Prospero rightly fears, as well as is attracted to, his delicate spirit, that part of him which must work, and work rightly, or the whole enterprise will be lost. He is really not in control at all, but in great jeopardy, because he is dependent upon the proper behavior of Ariel and the minor spirits, of Ferdinand and Miranda, of Alonzo and his entourage, and upon keeping Caliban in check; for if his charms do crack, if his ministers (who are also instruments of Fate and ministers of Destiny) fail to induce a genuine repentance, Prospero will not be able to achieve the self-absolving grace of forgiveness either. Ariel must keep the sinners alive that they might repent, "Or else his project dies"; the spectators at the masque must be silent, "Or else our spell is marred."

Although attended all the way by misgivings and anxious moments, Prospero's high charms do work, with the corroboration of godlike elegance in a destructive act: "Bravely the figure of this harpy hast thou Performed, my Ariel, a grace it had, devouring." Puck—that other air drinker, that unregenerate chameleon who could find and leave mortals only fools, who was best pleased with things that befall preposterously, who could bestow only a mixed blessing upon still bemused and insecurely sacramented lovers— has evolved into a beneficent sprite, through Prospero's tenacity, which denies Ariel freedom until he has become transformed, almost humanized, almost incarnated. In a brilliant reversal of Hamlets' self-damning comparison between the player, who *could* feel

for Hecuba, and himself, Shakespeare has Ariel, in the act of reporting to Prospero that his charm has so worked the sinners that
they suffer and repent, transfer to Prospero, through Ariel's new-
found capacity for tenderness, the ability to undergo a passion and
thus forgive himself. Prospero hastens to divest himself of his
powers, trusting for absolution through embracing the dynamics of
dissolution. Yet, at the very end in the epilogue, he must pray for
mercy and indulgence or else again, still, "his project fails," and he
himself will not be set free.

Several critics have recently pointed out the untransformed alloy
still in Prospero's assumption of virtuous godlike forgiveness: he is
grudging and less than gracious in promulgating his sovereign pardon; he snubs Miranda's outburst of wonderment at the beauty of
mankind; he puts conditions on his amnesty; he adopts, rather
Hamlet-like, a self-righteous attitude, siding with "nobler reason"
against the fury to which he feels entitled; and he opts for "virtue"
rather than (godlike) "vengeance" because it is "the rarer action." Prospero's words of "forgiveness" to *his* brother

> For you, most wicked sir, whom to call brother
> Would even infect my mouth, I do forgive
> Thy rankest fault—all of them—and require
> My dukedom of thee, which perforce I know
> Thou must restore

are reminiscent of Edgar's to Edmund and provoke a like uneasiness about the kind and degree of charity our hero has achieved.
The play is still full of such telltale qualifiers; let us just briefly go
into one of the least worked-over scenes, the masque of Ceres, for
internal, poetic-daemonic evidence of this strain of discord, which
is an inseparable part of the heavenly music that overcomes the
tempest.

First, note the corroboration that the entire action of the play is
taking place in Prospero's mind, in his reply to Ferdinand's polite
praise of the masque: "This is a most majestic vision, and Harmo-
nious charmingly. May I be bold To think these spirits?" Encour-

aged by this testimony to the success of his charms, Prospero responds, "Spirits which by mine art I have from their confines called *To enact my present fancies.*" Here we are at the heart and core of the perilous imaginative enterprise: calling from their containers the things normally contained, to give his vision of good a local habitation and a name. If he can embody his moral imagination at its present state of majesty combined with harmony, bringing the gods down to bless the earth, then his "tricks" are more substantial than merely "some vanity of his art." "Let me live here ever," says Ferdinand, "So rare a wonderful father and a wise Makes this place Paradise." But it is just here that Juno and Ceres "whisper seriously" and enact the really dangerous fancy: the temperate water nymphs are to dance with, to *encounter,* some representative men of earth, who are curiously selected. Not only are they sunburned and weary of August, but they are sicklemen, reapers, cutters-down, ominously reminiscent of the grimmest reaper of all.[48] Ceres has just sung her blessing, "Spring come to you at the farthest In the very end of harvest"—and here again the goddesses (Prospero's fanciful projections, remember) try to make these particular odds all even, by enforcing gracefulness, the dance, upon the encounter between natural antipathies. But it *fails;* this high charm does not work. The unexorcised thought of Caliban, the really uncultivated earth-fish-monster, reinvades Prospero's mind; the charming harmony becomes a "strange, hollow, and confused noise," and the spirits *heavily* vanish. We should note (as is not always remembered) that the famous melting, dissolving, rounded-with-a-sleep speech, which follows, is spoken from a troubled brain during Prospero's greatest crisis, his agon of passion, where he actually has to walk a turn or two to still his beating mind. He summons Ariel "with a thought," Ariel who "cleaves to his thought." Caliban has penetrated his mind, uncalled for and unwelcome.

Once this subtle but controlling emphasis is perceived, as it must be in the sudden, overt, dramatic start of Prospero, one can trace its reverberations backwards as well as forwards. Ceres and Juno have been carefully chosen to represent the good goddesses, and Iris has officiously excluded Venus and Cupid, Mars's hot minion and her waspish-headed son—in themselves telltale qualms about the efficacy of the procedure. Nor can even the crudest, unmitigated aspects of Ceres's kingdom on earth—spongy April; cold nymphs; the shadow that the dismissed bachelor loves, being lass-lorn; the sea marge, sterile and rocky-hard; bosky acres and unshrubbed down—be kept out of the invocation of so-called rich and bounteous Ceres. These attributes are there in the poetry; indeed, they are dominant. Prospero's (and Shakespeare's?) wishful reason summons up a vision of bounty, "some donation freely to estate On the blest lovers"; the subversive critic from the confines of the fancy (which has to produce the images) provides a largely sterile and rocky-hard landscape.

I would conclude with the suggestion that even here, at his most romantic and comico-magical, Shakespeare was loyal to his darker side and did wrestle mightily to the end. Like Jacob, he *was* given his vision of good, a ladder whereby earth and high heaven connected and interchanged. But he had to make a long journey, and struggle and labor and wait and connive and fear and fail, in his mission as spokesman and achiever for the dark gods at the top; and he had to wrestle all night, with his thigh (and the time) out of joint, and hang on, before he could prevail and be blessed. He had seen God face-to-face and had been preserved. He still was not told God's name, and he could not call it clear. But he gave the name of the place of wrestling, and it has remained not for an age but for all time: it is Shakespeare's tragic poetry.

3

Conrad: Romance and Tragedy

THESE EXPLORATIONS OF THE FORM AND FEATURE OF tragedy began with the suggestion that there is a within as well as a without to it, a hard core of negative capacity, a thing contained as well as containers, which is often obscured or distorted in the process of responding to, and even of creating, what we call tragedies. It is this thing, ultimately daemonic and autonomous, which constitutes the inner classic form of tragedy and which we must try to penetrate to and discern if we are to grasp the tragic well and truly. I proposed a formula—a diminutive form—which found counterparts as tune or rhythm within the executive forms; I tried to show Shakespeare constantly returning to and grappling with this masked challenger, being loyal to the instinct which told him it was both profound and most humanly, though mysteriously, significant: Shakespeare as inquisitor and critic. Now we might look at a later, and this time romantically inclined, writer who was possessed by the daemon and who used a different executive form, the novel. The question will be, Can tragedy serve—and be found trustworthy by—a teller of tales?

A hundred years ago, Unamuno's "tragic sense of life in men and peoples" seemed to have been lost, or nearly so. Four years before Conrad was born, Matthew Arnold could only look wistfully back at the time "Before this strange disease of modern life, With its sick hurry, its divided aimes, Its heads o'er taxed, its palsied hearts, Was rife"; his own day, he felt, was lived by "Light half-believers of our casual creeds, Who never deeply felt, nor clearly willed." Two years before Conrad was born, Arnold asked forgiveness of the masters of the mind for "Wandering between two worlds, one dead, The other powerless to be born." And, insofar as he was talking about an English world of tragedy (I believe he was, partly), he appears to have been right, for another half-century anyway. The Victorian compromise held sway wherever scientific progressivism halted. In literature, it was the heyday of the novel, which had long since filled the vacuum left by the disappearance of serious drama; and the novel, while certainly capable of dealing with tragic themes and ideas, in the hands of its greatest practitioners proved to be too much of an all-purpose form and too hospitable to ethical realism to serve or generate a major tragedy. Morton Zabel sums it up: "The Victorian novel had expanded, explored, digressed, moralized, and conquered"; but it had reached that "impasse of demoralization" which was waiting at the summit of its own treacherous empiricism. Hawthorne's felt need for a return to the romance-origin of the novel, with its grounding in mystery and its affinity with the powers of darkness, was instrumental in shaping the fruitful, but not fully realized, tragic potential in classic American literature—Lawrence's mordant "Studies" therein make the point over and over; and there apparently was real danger of European romanticism's degenerating into what W. J. Cash has called "the cardboard medievalism of the Scotch novels." It might be said that by the end of the century tragedy was in need of a romantic with a vision of evil who could write novels in English about the predicament of the modern European; and fortuitously at this very point Conrad—a polylingual Pole turned Englishman who had penetrated the capitals of Europe, the seven seas, the British Empire, and the heart of darkest Africa—left the bridge of his ship and sat down to his desk for thirty years of doing just that.[1]

Conrad is here proposed, then, as exemplary of the romantic ethos of tragedy, and we shall examine what has been called the paradigm of his central theme, *Lord Jim*, for evidences of the astringent therapeutic power of the tragic core over the tendency of romantic open form to maudlin dilation, and for assurances that his underlying honesty and loyalty to the hard tragic vision saved him from muscular Stoicism and moral complacency. There will also be glimpses of that cross-referencing and reinforcement from the past and contemporary masters of the mind which are our best guarantee that what we perceive and respond to in tragic masterpieces is true, and not self-induced, frivolous, or ephemeral.

R. M. Adams, in his study of open form, finds that literary openness generally operates in the service of the critical spirit—"a tribute to the reality principle, and, perhaps more particularly, to the supreme form of that sinister impulse the death wish." "Art is eternal, but it is not true; it is a higher form of truth, but we must be teased into it and cannot remain long under its influence."[2] (In *Lord Jim*, when Jewel insists that Jim was false, Stein cries "No! No! Not false. True! True! True! . . . You don't understand." And what the simple-minded girl cannot understand is the tragic fact that truth is deadlier than "falseness.") We find, when Nietzsche's sorceress has us in thrall, that "in notions not only lovely but familiar, it seems horrid possibilities may lurk." "The symbol, as allegory and object, looks two ways and exists in an essential tension."[3] The telltale signs of open form—ambivalence, conceit, *trompe-l'oeil*, authorial detachment or irony—can be found, Adams demonstrates, in all kinds of works and in all periods; but he moves toward two generic attitudes and forms, epic and romance, as archetypal of the closed and the open. The epic codifies and organizes, "summarizes the familiar"; the romance "extends experience instead of compacting it." "Yet," he concludes, "the relation between these two forms is not truly antithetical but complementary; epic codifies and imposes values on a world which romance explores and enlarges." Some of us would dispute such a reductionist view of epic, finding the recalcitrant tragic antinomies strewn through even the most establishmentarian of sagas; but the idea is a fruitful one all the same and can lead us to a perception of like relation—antithetical and at the same time complementary—between romance and tragedy.

Conrad provides us with our text, the well-known statement from the Author's Note to *Within the Tides*, which was cited in the first chapter:

> The romantic feeling of reality was in me an inborn faculty. This in itself may be a curse, but, when disciplined by a sense of personal responsibility and a recognition of the hard facts of existence shared with the rest of mankind, becomes but a point of view from which the very shadows of life appear endowed with an internal glow. And such romanticism is not a sin. It is none the worse for the knowledge of truth. It only tries to make the best of it, hard as it may be; and in this hardness discovers a certain aspect of beauty.[4]

Curse, sin, shadows of life, none the worse, make the best of it, hardness—the rocks are there, as in Ceres' invocation in *The Tempest*, all over this determinedly glowing landscape. And, from *A Personal Record*, there is another willful testimonial:

> The ethical view of the universe involves us at last in so many cruel and absurd contradictions, where the last vestiges of faith, hope, charity, and even of reason itself, seem ready to perish, that I have come to suspect that the aim of creation cannot be ethical at all. I would fondly believe that its object is purely spectacular; a spectacle for awe, love, adoration, or hate, if you like, but in this view—and in this view alone—never for despair! . . . our conscience [is] gifted with a voice in order to bear true testimony to the visible wonder, the haunting terror, the infinite passion, and the illimitable serenity; to the supreme law and the abiding mystery of the sublime spectacle.[5]

This is official romanticism with a vengeance, beating the adjectival drums with insistency; but it was called into play by the nagging suspicion, which would not down, that our desire for reason and ethics, when thwarted, does lure us to despair.

And, to complicate it all further, Conrad was a romantic not against but for and about values: he repudiated the reputation of rebel or revolutionary and embraced the posh British Empire code so warmly that it embarrassed even some of his adopted countrymen. Yet, in his artistic life, he was a confirmed open-former; *Lord Jim*, he tells us, was to have been, and indeed started out to be, "a free and wandering tale," which "could conceivably colour the whole 'sentiment of existence' in a simple and sensitive character."[6] (Zabel has epitomized this much-discussed aspect of Conrad's art as the "intricate means of indirection . . . the empirical, cross-chronological, cumulative, and incremental method."[7]) The difference here seems to be that, in addition to the kinds of romantic openness which Adams cites[8]—Whitman, Lawrence,[9] Faulkner, Virginia Woolf, Jack Kerouac, for examples—Conrad provides another variant, which *uses* the fluidity of openness, and recognizes its inherent negativism, in the avowed interests of achieving positiveness and solidarity—the aspect of beauty *in* the hardness. It is wrestling with the angel, again, but differently from Shakespeare (who escaped the deadlock, I suggest, by making *Antony and Cleopatra* a triumph of fluidity over solidity) in that the business is done consciously, out in the open, heart-on-sleeve.

I will cite a few more of Conrad's remarks in this vein for a framework from outside the novels. From the preface to *The Nigger of the Narcissus:* "Confronted by the same enigmatical spectacle, the artist descends within himself, and in that lonely region of stress and strife, if he is deserving and fortunate, he finds the terms of his appeal." Fiction, the mode of being of Sidney's poet "who nothing affirmeth, and therefore never lieth," was Conrad's chosen way of life and expression; yet he could assert, "The sustained invention of a really telling lie demands a talent which I do not possess." He again protested (in *A Personal Record*) that giving in to passion, "like an actor who raises his voice above the pitch of natural conversation," though an unwelcome and dangerous necessity for an artist who would move others deeply, "surely is no great sin." "Creative effort," for a sensibility like Conrad's, "is a strain . . . in which mind and will and conscience are engaged to the full, hour after hour, day after day . . . like the everlasting sombre stress of the westward winter passage round Cape Horn." "One admires what one lacks. This is why I admire perseverance and fidelity and constancy."[10] This is closer to a modern reincarnation of the Hamlet conception than, say, Porfiry's attribution to the young Russian romantics, in *Crime and Punishment*—the author himself as tragic hero, who wants in his heart of heart to be *not* passion's slave, but who knows that he must, like an actor, in a fiction, in a dream of passion, like a whore unpack his heart with words. *Surely*, Conrad kept pleading, this is not meretricious, not a sin. Kenneth Muir reminds us that "Shakespeare created Hamlet, but Hamlet created Shakespeare."[11] Conrad, in addition to re-creating parts of himself in dozens of characters, found it necessary to produce a literary alter-ego (Marlow), an intermediary tale-teller who could help him take the strain and stress and undergo some of the ordeal and agon of a romantic heart confronted by a tragic vision. It was the Marlow of *Lord Jim* who was able to pronounce Jim "one of us,"[12] before Conrad himself could say the words, in the Author's Note written long after the fact, *in propria persona.*

This unpacking his heart with words undergoes, in *Lord Jim*, an anguished attenuation, which often bids fair to defeat its own purpose and alienate the readers Conrad was so desperate to make "hear, feel, and *see*." Marlow enters the original third-person narrative as a character—an interested spectator in the courtroom—then takes over the tale-telling to the men on the verandah, among whom is Conrad (though unidentified and still in the third person), "the only one man of all these listeners who was ever to hear the last word of the story." This tragically "privileged man" heard it, and felt it, through seeing, reading the packet which contained the narrative itself, enclosed in Marlow's still further attempt to explain and Jim's even more abortive attempt to "Tell them!" Containers within containers are laid on; and it is a painfully contorted—or contortionist's—kind of struggling, which discloses something close to our formula when Marlow reports it: " 'No,' Jim concluded, 'Nothing.' That was all then—and there shall be nothing more; there shall be no message, unless such as each of us can interpret for himself from the language of facts, that are so often more enigmatic than the craftiest arrangement of words." We, drawn by now into this involved kind of team-wrestling match, are to take it that Jim tried his best to say the word, to "deliver himself," but failed; Marlow then took it up, and (as we shall see later on) first left Jim's story an enigma, tried again, and even at the end, "like an evoked ghost," wondered and said, "Who knows?" So *Conrad* goes in and re-creates it all over again, summoning those shadowy realities from within his ghostly heart. The crafty arrangement of words is our conscious artist, the codifier and organizer, Nietzsche's Apollonian genius; the language of facts is what comes out of the mouth of the enigmatic Dionysian demon when invoked to speak. Marlow puts this recognition of the ascendancy of the hard tragic over the willful romantic most succinctly near the end of his letter handing over the baton, as it were, to the next contestant:

I put it down here for you as though I had been an eye-witness. . . .
You must admit that it is romantic beyond the wildest dreams of his
boyhood, and yet there is to my mind a sort of profound and terrify-
ing logic in it, as if it were our imagination alone that could set loose
upon us the might of an overwhelming destiny.

Conrad's dream of romantic sentiment has been confronted by the fact of tragic logic and has acquiesced therein.

One of the great dialectical axes of any tragic view of life is the reality-illusion axis, and it is an earnest of Conrad's solid grounding in the tragic that he uses these terms, unabashedly, at all times and in any connection; he was constantly probing their natures and matching them up with two other large categories of meaning for man as a moral agent, good and evil. What makes the dialectic fruitful is that the pairings can, and do, shift: truth, we say, is autonomous and must therefore be good; man's moral integrity is destroyed by a lie. But when we approach truth or reality it turns out to be inhuman, appalling, transcendent or destructive to all lesser goods and hence, in ordinary humanistic terms, evil. Illusion is to be fought and contemned, because it informs those patently evil and unhuman activities which Conrad constantly castigates as folly, delusion, lugubrious drollery, imbecility, farce, insanity; it is the worst of evils, the consort of rapacity and pitilessness. Yet without dreams, idealisms, and those peculiarly Conradian constructions Deliberate Belief and Surface Truth, there can be no beauty in human action— and the beautiful is also the good.

As a thinker, Conrad could be demonstrated to be an almost thoroughgoing agnostic, or at least a stoic. His letters, his essays, his autobiographical musings, his critical prefaces and notes strike a consistent note of skepticism. Let this serve as typical (from a letter to Cunningham Graham, in 1898—the year of the beginning of *Lord Jim*):

> Of course reason is hateful,—but why? Because it demonstrates (to those who have the courage) that we, living, are out of life,—utterly out of it. The mysteries of a universe made of drops of fire and clods of mud do not concern us in the least. The fate of a humanity condemned ultimately to perish from cold is not worth troubling about. If you take it to heart it becomes an unendurable tragedy. If you believe in improvement you must weep, for the attained perfection must end in cold, darkness, and silence. In a dispassionate view the ardour for reform, improvement, for virtue, for knowledge and even for beauty is only a vain sticking up for appearances, as though one were anxious about the cut of one's clothes in a community of blind men.

Life knows us not and we do not know life,—we don't know even our own thoughts. Half the words we use have no meaning whatever and of the other half each man understands each word after the fashion of his own folly and conceit. Faith is a myth and beliefs shift like mists on the shore: thoughts vanish: words, once pronounced, die: only the string of my platitude seems to have no end. As our peasants say, "Pray, brother, forgive me for the love of God." And we don't know what forgiveness is, nor what is love, nor where God is. *Assez!*[13]

This is a vision of evil under the aspect of vanity which is as old as *Ecclesiastes* and as new as the age of science; one marvels that anyone who could be impelled to state it could also write novels about human solidarity. Embracing it qualifies Conrad, however, as a spokeman for the post-Renaissance humanist, for it can be a surrogate for the Manichaeism we are able to attribute to ages of faith as a recognition of metaphysical evil. Conrad had no real conception of the supernatural as good or bad; and even in his imaginative works, where he seeks for an objective correlative to the forces operating in the human heart, the images remain naturalistic and do not get much beyond the theatricality of the pathetic fallacy (an earthquake rumbles in the wings to validate the catastrophe in *Victory;* to accompany the statement in *Lord Jim* that we are "being made to comprehend the Inconceivable," we are provided with "That side of which, like the other hemisphere of the moon, exists stealthily in perpetual darkness, with only a fearful ashy light falling at times on the edge.") His widest overplot seems to be some kind of dimly perceived moral universe, a solidarity with mankind that is the end aim of what Zabel calls "that moral teleology of humanity which must be the novel's supreme theme and problem."[14] Conrad was in the condition of the modern man of good will who still believed in original sin (or at least in the devastation it has had on human nature) without the counter-balancing reassurance of a rational faith in the Redemption. This agnosticism and skepticism, then, stood him in good stead in keeping faith, through at least two-thirds of his work, with the profoundly sombre view of man's nature and destiny which we are drawn to and admire in the tragedian. Melville said, "The mortal man who hath more of joy than sorrow in him, that mortal man cannot be true"; he would doubtless agree that Conrad was "fitted to sit down on tombstones, and break the green damp mould with unfathomably wondrous Solomon"—that is, Ecclesiastes, "the fine hammered steel of woe."

Before hurrying on to the other side to balance the picture, one could make, I believe, a suggestive case for Conrad as the writer who set the tone for some modern, partially tragic treatments of man's predicament. If T. S. Eliot and Scott Fitzgerald may be said (despite Eliot's disclaimer) to have expressed the tragic insights and frustrations of a generation, then perhaps we might lay claim to Conrad as our spokesman too: he in his turn becomes "one of *us*."

There are innumerable connections among these three; we can mention just a few. The famous "waste land" phrase and image— the shore and the river—crop up in *Lord Jim* and in *The Great Gatsby*. Eliot brought out *The Hollow Men* in 1925, introducing, ultimately, thousands of new readers to *Heart of Darkness* with the epigraph, "Mr. Kurtz—he dead." Conrad, through Marlow, says that though Kurtz was "hollow to the core," he had escaped the "impalpable greyness" of "tepid skepticism"; he was a "remarkable man"—at least he was a violent lost soul, not an Arnoldian dweller in the antechamber of Hell. Conrad admired Baudelaire and saluted him in an epigraph; Eliot's essay on Baudelaire expatiates on the paradox of a kind of redemption through thoroughgoing damnation. Fitzgerald concluded that "the natural state of the sentient adult is a qualified unhappiness"; Conrad had said, "the only one of our feelings for which it is impossible to become a sham" is "resignation open-eyed, conscious, and informed by love." Gatsby "turned out all right in the end"—as did not the hollow people who "preyed on him"—because of his "capacity for wonder," "the colossal vitality of his illusion"; Kurtz's fiancée was preserved by a "great and saving illusion."[15] In *The Waste Land*, out on the Thames (not the dull canal) there are these antithetical sights and memories:

The river sweats	Elizabeth and Leicester
Oil and tar	Beating oars
The barges drift	The stern was formed
With the turning tide	A gilded shell
Red sails	Red and gold
Wide	The brisk swell
To leeward, swing on the heavy spar.	Rippled both shores
The barges wash	Southwest wind
Drifting logs	Carried down stream
Down Greenwich reach	The peal of bells
Past the Isle of Dogs.	White towers.

Sweet Thames, run softly, till I end my song.

O city, city.   I had not thought death had undone so many.

Now listen to the setting—first and last—of *Heart of Darkness:*

The *Nellie*, a cruising yawl, swung to her anchor . . . to wait for the turn of the tide. The sea-reach of the Thames stretched before us . . . the tanned sails of the barges drifting up with the tide seemed to stand still in red clusters of canvas sharply peaked, with gleams of varnished spirits. . . . The air was dark above Gravesend, and farther back still seemed condensed into mournful gloom, brooding motionless over the biggest, and the greatest, town on earth. . . . The offing was barred by a black bank of clouds, and the tranquil waterway leading to the uttermost ends of the earth flowed somber under an overcast sky—seemed to lead into the heart of an immense darkness. . . . And at last, in its curved and imperceptible fall, the sun sank low, . . . as if about to go out suddenly, stricken to death by the touch of the gloom brooding over a crowd of men.

Forthwith a change came over the waters. . . . Nothing is easier . . . than to evoke the great spirit of the past upon the lower reaches of the Thames . . . from Sir Francis Drake to Sir John Franklin, knights all, titled and untitled—the great knight-errants of the sea. It had borne all the ships whose names are like jewels flashing in the night

of time, from the *Golden Hind* returning with her round flanks full
of treasure, to be visited by the Queen's Highness and thus pass out
of the gigantic tale. . . . And further west on the upper reaches the
place of the monstrous town was still marked ominously on the sky,
a brooding gloom in sunshine, a lurid glare under the stars.

"And this also," said Marlow suddenly, "has been one of the dark
places of the earth."

If Pound was for the early Eliot *il miglior fabbro*, his best tutor in
poetics, Conrad might be said to have been his tragic mentor: Eliot,
who wrote to Fitzgerald about *Gatsby*, "It has interested and ex-
cited me more than any novel I have seen, either English or American, for a number of years . . . it seems to me such a remarkable
book . . . the first step that American fiction has taken since Henry
James"; Fitzgerald, who included among "imitators of Conrad,"
"Me in *Gatsby*. God! I've learned a lot from him."[16] We note here
not only echoes of Conrad's seminal images of wasteland and civi-
lized darkness but also the gleam of the romantic spirit which he
perhaps alone was able to salvage from *fin de siècle* boredom and
nihilism: "Inexplicable splendour of Ionian white and gold," but
splendor nevertheless; and Gatsby's "Platonic conception of himself," in which he went about his business in "the service of a vast,
vulgar, meretricious beauty," "to which conception he was faithful
to the end." As Stein said of Jim and all romantics: "*Ewig—usque
ad finem.*" An ingrained, if never quite explicable, idealism was the
other side of Conrad's greatness.[17]

Taken by itself, this romantic ethos found outlet in many of
Conrad's stories—in his enchantment with the sea, with the exoti-
cism of the Orient; in his revolutionary impetuosity; in his warm
empathy with the generosity of youth and youths. But for our
purpose it is important to notice that he seldom gave in, at any
length, to the uncritical romanticism which would result in tales
merely picaresque or picturesque. Chance and opportunity are indeed indispensable—they are mysteriously connected with truth—
and the positive affirmation and commitment, the grasp, the leap,

are the constant dynamics of Conrad's vision of human life. But one must not only, in Stein's celebrated phrase, "in the destructive element immerse," in order to be, one must also "make the deep, deep sea keep you up." And this involves exertions; it involves cost, the disconcerting and sickening realization that the element, the "external and objective reality in which men are fated to live," is "a perilous disequilibrium of [humanity's] moral and spiritual forces." Romanticism, like pessimism, can get out of hand; and even, rarely, the two can be combined in the wrong way and go sour: I find *Victory* a failure as tragedy because, as Zabel says, Heyst's "untested misanthropy is as fatally romantic a presumption on the conditions of the responsible life or the obligations of character as an untested optimism."[18] When Conrad theorized about tragicalness (with the journalistic use of the terms), or strained after it, I think he failed also. Witness the overblown and (in the story) unsubstantiated statement about Jim and Jewel: "These few sounds wandering the dark had made their two benighted lives tragic to my mind. . . . They had mastered their fates. They were tragic."

But *Nostromo*, the next big novel after *Lord Jim*, hits out many approximations of our tragic formula, showing that the daemon is in there striking shrewd blows: there is "something inherent in the necessities of successful action which carries with it the moral degradation of the idea"; "It was impossible to disentangle one's activity from its debasing contacts"; "The cruel futility of lives and deaths thrown away in the vain endeavor to attain an enduring solution of the problem"; "His vanity was infinitely and naively greedy, but his conceptions were limited." Decoud was "a victim of the disillusioned weariness which is the retribution meted out to intellectual audacity"; Nostromo himself was "a victim of the disenchanted vanity which is the reward of audacious action." Success is failure.

And, when romanticism and pessimism *are* balanced and placed in the true tragic dialectic, then Conrad produces something which comes as close as we have a right to expect to a tragedy in the novel form. We say that tragedy is consummated when the dream of innocence is confronted by the fact of guilt and acquiesces therein. I should like to try to use *Lord Jim* as a paradigm of this action, because it not only has some of the best Conradian texts on the subject but also shows that rare achievement of form which is the merging of the dream and the fact. One of Conrad's chief visions of good was fidelity, often called solidarity, "the solidarity in mysterious origin, in toil, in joy, in hope, in uncertain fate, which binds men to each other." To prove himself one of and with his fellowmen was Jim's dream of innocence, his shadowy ideal of heroic conduct; "and yet is not mankind itself, pushing on its blind way, driven by a dream of its greatness and its power upon the dark path of excessive cruelty and of excessive devotion. And what is the pursuit of truth, after all?"[19] And it was in the very terms of brotherhood that the unspeakable Gentleman Brown forced Jim's collaboration in the destruction of all he valued and the sacrifice of his life. It has the tremendous inevitability, the rightness, of the classic tragic fusion of the truthful with the hateful.

But it was not inevitable from the beginning. As we have noted, Conrad began with a "free and wandering tale" which "could conceivably colour the whole 'sentiment of existence' in a simple and sensitive character." That is, *Lord Jim* was originally to be freely romantic; and, I believe, it originally moved towards a wholly romantic, and hence unsatisfactory, close. For there are two endings to *Lord Jim*, and a conjectural reconstruction of how this came about will be instructive of the profoundly rooted tragic spirit in Conrad.

Marlow's spoken narrative ends with the tableau of Tuan Jim on the beach, white-clad, "with the stronghold of the night at his back, the sea at his feet, the opportunity at his side." He and the two natives he was acting as a father to were "in luck." He had won his fight; he had told Marlow that he was satisfied—nearly. This was a triumph few men achieved, and it was enough—almost. Marlow's misgivings about the veil still on the opportunity-bride are for the moment overcome by the tour de force of the scene, the tableau. But the book (as we have it now) doesn't end there, and the narrative form changes significantly: the romantic tale now comes to a close with the swift-moving, last-act tragic rush of a tightly dramatizable action, culminating in Jim's final perception of his bride-ideal unveiled, at the precise moment of his complete renunciation. The truth has made him free, and dead. He has at last been equal to the occasion and has found an occasion worthy of his allegiance. How did this come to be? To account for it would take a whole analysis of *Heart of Darkness*, of Marlow, of Conrad's Congo experience, and of his attempt to purge himself of it by writing it out of him ten years after it happened; here I can just sketch a theory.[20]

After the Dostoievskian "double," perhaps the most important modern contribution to the tragic method has been the idea of the author as hero, the bearer of the burden of truth. (Look forward, for a moment, from Marlow to Fitzgerald's Nick Carraway, the narrator in *Gatsby*, who did not succeed in preserving his detachment in the presence of "privileged glimpses into the human heart"; to Tiresias of *The Waste Land*, who has foresuffered all enacted in his story, has perceived, foretold, "throbbing between two lives.") Marlow had become involved with Jim, all right, in the first part of the tale, but he was unsatisfied with what he had been able to do and hear and see and say: "That was my last view of him— in a strong light, dominating, and yet in complete accord with his surroundings—with the life of the forests and with the life of man." Yet, "For me that white figure in the stillness of coast and sea seemed to stand in the heart of a vast enigma." And the demon surges to the surface with the reason:

Finis! The Pacific is the most discreet of live, hot tempered oceans. . . . And there is a sense of blessed finality in such discretion, which is what we all more or less sincerely are ready to admit—for what else is it that makes the idea of death supportable? End! Finis! the potent word that exorcises from the house of life the haunting shadow of fate. This is what—notwithstanding the testimony of my

eyes and his own earnest assurances—I miss when I look back upon
Jim's success. While there's life there is hope, truly; but there is fear,
too. I don't mean to say that I regret my action, nor will I pretend
that I can't sleep o'nights in consequence; still the idea obtrudes itself
that he made so much of his disgrace while it is the guilt alone that
matters. He was not—if I may so—clear to me. He was not clear. And
there is the suspicion that he was not clear to himself either.

The Marlow of *Youth*, who, though "entranced as if before a profound, a fateful enigma," exulted "like a conqueror" and found out
"how good a man he was," had not plunged into the really destructive element at all. So, he became the protagonist of *Heart of
Darkness;* took up the burden of discovery; made his descent into
hell; sought out Kurtz in the very heart of evil; went through the
ordeal of the journey, the debasing collaboration with folly (armed
only lightly with his surface truth), and the struggle with Kurtz's
demonic soul; saw the Gorgon face of appalling truth; heard the
blasphemous affirmation; made his choice of nightmares; and
dreamed it out to the end, *usque ad finem.* More, he did not end on
the high note of Kurtz's abominable victory, the bespeaking of "the
horror"; this would have been romantic indeed, like Byron's
Gothic Manfred. No, Marlow was loyal to Kurtz, and he went
back to Europe, "surrendered personally," purged himself of realities, paid for his experience by the bitter loss of his integrity: he
told The Intended a lie. And it was a tragic catharsis, for the dull
anger that stirred in him "subsided before a feeling of infinite pity,"
when he perceived the solidarity between her luminous illusion, the
only light left in a darkening world, and the deliberate belief,
abominable as it was, of her champion of the darkness, Kurtz. The
dream of romantic illusory innocence had merged in umbrageous
beauty with the hard truth of reality, with the fact of guilt. And so
Marlow-Conrad returned to *Lord Jim* and with a marvelously
quickened touch brought his romantic hero to his tragic consum-
mation.[21]
    During the long recital, by means of distorted chronology and

incremental repetition, of Jim's struggle toward romantic success, the softened version of antagonism prevails; Jim's dream has come "into violent collision with public circumstance." But this too is whistling in the graveyard; he (and Marlow) remain unclear. They both know that somehow they have not really got hold of the heart of the darkness: Jim's heroism is symbolized by a carefully and deliberately invested whiteness "that seemed to catch all the light left in a darkened world," but it was a twilight tableau, softened at the edges—gleam against gloom, not blackness. The emergence of Gentleman Brown, full-grown and demonically vital, into Conrad's conscious executive form from the depths where he had been lurking changed all that when "at last, running his appointed course, he sails into Jim's history, a blind accomplice of the Dark Powers."

In countless details Brown is the obverse of Jim, Mephistophilis to his Faust, not the clear recognizable enemy. All the circumstances, the motives, the ideals of Jim's life are reflected in Brown and called by their stark right names. He had deserted from a home ship; his luck had left him; he became a freebooter, a buccaneer; he was blackmailing the native villages along the coast. He was tired of his life and not afraid of death, but stood in mortal fear of imprisonment—was running away from the spectre of a Spanish prison. He found his way at last to, and his golden opportunity at, Patusan, penetrating it at the exact same place where Jim had landed. He has earned an epithet for himself, Gentleman Brown, as his counterpart has become Tuan Jim, and has called himself proudly the Scourge of God. Exacerbated by failure, ill luck, and privation, he showed an undisguised ruthlessness of purpose, a strange vengeful attitude toward his own past; and one could perceive that what he had really desired, almost in spite of himself, was to play havoc with that jungle town. He accepted the disappointing course of events with a sulky obstinacy, never giving up his fixed idea.[22]

Jim's life was the dream, Brown's the fact; and Marlow-Conrad, in forcing the identity to the almost too obvious extreme, has them meet in the agon of confrontation "on the very spot where Jim took the second desperate leap of his life." Brown immediately seizes the initiative, throwing Jim's questions back at him with uncanny aptness ("I knew what to say," he boasts later) and reasserting again and again the essential likeness of their apparently opposite cases. He does not need to hear the story of Jim's life: "I know it is no better than mine. I've lived—and so did you though you talk as though you were one of those people that should have wings so as to go about without touching the dirty earth. Well—it is dirty. . . . I am here because I was afraid once in my life." Jim stands his ground under the initial assault, silently absorbing the massive injection of poison. It is masterly technique, having all this come to the reader by way of Marlow respeaking and interpreting Brown's words and perceiving thereby that Jim is acknowledging it as the truth about his own life: he cannot stop Brown from speaking for him; they are merging into one. "There ran," says Marlow, "through the rough talk a vein of subtle reference to their common blood, an assumption of common experience; a sickening suggestion of guilt, of secret knowledge that was like a bond of their minds and of their hearts." Jim makes one more small attempt to dictate the terms of the merger and is defeated by Brown. He throws away the switch he held in his hand and acquiesces: "Very well." Hamlet had said, "Let be." And, also like the last scenes of *Hamlet*, "Henceforth events move fast without a check, flowing from the very hearts of men like a stream from a dark source." But the real agon, the real tragic action, is already finished—and Marlow too gets almost the whole tragic perception:

> To me the conversation of those two across the creek appears now as the deadliest kind of duel on which Fate looked with her cold-eyed knowledge of the end. No, he didn't turn Jim's soul inside out, but I am much mistaken if the spirit so utterly out of his reach had not been made to taste to the full the bitterness of that contest.

Marlow-Conrad still wants to wrestle, and does so of course by creating Jim's heroic expiatory martyrdom, and calling it "an extraordinary success!" But he still fails to pin his protean adversary.

What *was* Jim's purpose, his dream of innocence? Altruism, solidarity with mankind—Timon's philanthropy. He had been able to pursue it and apparently achieve it—almost—by single-minded, pertinacious, epic-heroic endeavor, consolidating his gains, building his stronghold. He called it The Fort, Patusan. But even here, ominously under the "alluring shape of such an extraordinary success" (the bitch goddess), loom the tell-tale hard structural bones of a Tower of Babel. "It was an excellent plan, . . . a place of safety" showing "his judicious foresight, his faith in the future. . . . Within he would be an invincible host in himself." And when he tried to write to the world from this position, heading the message "The Fort, Patusan," the pen spluttered, and he "gave it up." Acquiesced. The hard core of tragic intransigeance, the very root of evil, had come out in Gentleman Brown, called twice by Marlow by its true name: "mad self-love" and "almost inconceivable egotism"; now at the very end—by dint of the return to the rush of heroic narrative?—it is euphemized to "superb egoism" and "exalted egoism" when it is returned to Jim as an accolade. Good night, sweet Tuan! and go bid the soldiers shoot.

But this is the Hollywood ending; and Conrad, as we said at the beginning, though willfully romantic, was loyal to the tragic sense, and he could not let his tragic experience in the dark heart of man end on a trumped-up note of affirmation. Jim's real test, his real pathos—and for that matter Marlow's—did not come until the confrontation with Brown. And the perception was a tragic one: that altruism is egoism, egotism, solipsism; that excessive philanthropy is misanthropy; that truth is falsehood. "This above all," Polonius had babbled at the end of *his* platitudes, "To thine own self be true, And it must follow, as the night the day, Thou canst not be false to any man." It does indeed follow, by the absurd, dark-seeking logic of tragedy: day turns into night; *fiat lux, apparet umbra;* tragedy's charm might well be *Nox et Veritas*. Hamlet, we are beginning to see through the holes punched in the gabardine of humanism by the tragic monster underneath, had something of an obsessive Oedipal complex towards Polonius; and Hamlet, egoistically dedicated to achieving the integrity of his own dear soul, is a black-suited ambassador of death, "His liberty is full of threats to all." (Remember Adams's reminder that "Art is eternal but it is not true; it is a higher form of truth, but we must be teased into it and cannot remain long under its influence.") The minister of the ordinant heavens is a scourge to men. The Prince of Darkness is a gentleman. Gentleman Brown (too bad Conrad didn't call him Black, but perhaps he was striving for delicacy) is the alter-ego of Lord Jim. Jewel, enclosed in her own selfish world, stubbornly insists to the end that "he was false." Stein cries, "No! not false! True! True! . . . You don't understand." Stein understands, and finds it terrible; he cannot explain it to Jewel and will not explain it to Marlow. "And what is the pursuit of truth, after all?" When Jim persuaded the Patusani to let Brown go, "most of them simply said that 'they believed Tuan Jim.' In this simple form of assent to his will," Marlow comments, "lies the whole gist of the situation; their creed his truth; and the testimony to that faithfulness which made him in his own eyes the equal of the impeccable men who never fall out of the ranks. . . . 'Romantic!' " Yes, romantically true to his own self, tragically false to all men.

The rest is epiphany, and catharsis. "He had beheld the face of that opportunity which, like an Eastern bride, had come veiled to his side"; "he goes away from a living woman to celebrate his pitiless wedding with a shadowy ideal of conduct." Conrad was honest enough to strew in misgivings about Jim's success even all through the last heroic episode; Jewel does not forgive him and leads a "soundless, inert life"; Stein is saddened by her lack of perception and prepares "to leave all this." And Marlow-Conrad is openformed enough to be willing to end his tale with a question and a wonderment—Who knows? Jim is still inscrutable at heart.

It is a remarkable demonstration of the meeting of romance and tragedy, that East and West which are both antithetical and complementary. Conrad could not think his way, or believe his way, out of his vision of evil; but, armed with a romantic heart, he first lived it out, and then lived it again in writing it out, and tamed it by the art and the form of tragedy.

4

Faulkner: Saying No to Death

THE TROUBLE WITH "PROBING TO THE HEART OF radical nay saying," as Irving Howe declares a great deal of seemingly "excessive and morbid" literature does,[1] is that it is hard to stop. Both the nay and the saying find themselves caught up in a kind of soritic chain reaction, or infinite regress: C. S. Lewis's fissiparous-evil phenomenon.[2] And in the process one finds a range of strategies—from, say, Sidney's bravura attempt to turn his lady's "No, no, no, no, my love, let be" into a capitulation by way of the grammar rules which decree that a double negative brings about an affirmative, through Timon's wry "My long sickness Of health and living now begins to mend, And nothing brings me all things," to the direct attribution of the defect of its own virtue to the life-denying force itself—Donne's "Death, thou shalt die." Faulkner tries all the ways: the (perhaps) frenetic, self-indulgent, whiskey-inspired pronouncements of his programmatic executive stance, backed up by unremitting wrestlings with the demon in a lifetime of effort comparable in many ways to Shakespeare's and Conrad's.

In spite of his being an enigmatic figure and his offending the sensibilities of some readers, we can be confident of Faulkner's stature as a writer for many reasons: the sheer bulk and steadiness of his output; the massiveness and density of his style; the complexity *and* homogeneity of his creation, a whole field full of folk— Yoknapatawpha County, "William Faulkner, sole owner and proprietor." He has explained that "by sublimating the actual into the apocryphal I would have complete liberty to use whatever talent I might have to its absolute top. It opened up a gold mine of other people, so I created a cosmos of my own."[3] I find also (*pace* Hemingway)[4] a touchstone in his willing and unembarrassed use of big, polysyllabic, cosmic, abstract words, even in what seem to be trivial or ludicrous contexts: indomitable, intractable, infallible, relinquishment, repudiation, outrage, quenchless lucidity, destiny, the ding dong of doom. But the most convincing credentials lie in the *range* of his work, on the score of form and on the score of vision; and in the way his death wish (piety to the demon) is exercised and exorcised: not by saying No! in thunder, nor by reducing all language and rhetoric to Nada Nada Nada, but by containing it within a web loose enough that it can speak from its confinement and even have the last word. This is the mode of a tragedian.

Nonetheless, it is difficult to keep what the artist has fused into an imaginative unity from becoming an indistinguishable (and consequently undistinguished and feeble) blur for us, because Faulkner has embedded (contained?) his vertiginous intimations of mortality within the most opaque of the theological virtues—hope— and the most dogged version of its natural counterpart (fortitude), simple endurance. His programmatic statements, notably the Nobel Prize speech, are well enough known perhaps to allow one more to complete the record for our present purposes: in the *Reader* foreword he quotes "an old half-forgotten Pole": "This book was written at the expense of considerable effort, to uplift men's hearts"

and I thought: *What a nice thing to have thought to say* . . . still writing the books because they had to be written after the blood and glands began to slow and cool a little and the heart began to tell him, *You don't know the answer either and you will never find it,* but still writing the books because the demon was still kind; only a little more severe and unpitying . . . He would uplift man's heart for his own benefit because in that way he can say No to death. . . . At least we are not vegetables because the hearts and glands capable of partaking in this excitement are not those of vegetables, and will, must, endure.

It is much like what we have in Conrad and Yeats and Camus, a willed retort to rather than an understanding of the enigmatic demon within; and our task here is to identify the *douce adversaire,* the kind friend and severest critic who enabled Faulkner to negate nihilism with a *sursum corda* of his own peculiar devising. It largely resides in one or another version of the potent little phrase *at least:* in form, the superlative of littleness, next-to-nothing; but in virtue (like *if?*) it is much and can— at least!—tempt the dragon Nil out to where it will be recognized and defied, before acquiescing in its primacy and ultimacy.

He was certainly attracted to and fascinated by the genie in its suddenly enlarged dimensions when, polishing the lamp of his own genius, he evoked it to brood over his visionary landscape; it is a moot point among Faulknerians whether he managed to weave his loosely containing net fast and flexibly enough to control the sudden loomings and lurchings of its suffocating wings. (This is a daring and touchy business: remember Prospero's relief and exhilaration when he finds that his high charms do *work*—

> Bravely, the figure of this harpy hast thou
> Performed, my Ariel, a grace it had, devouring.)

Some critics have singled out *Absalom, Absalom!* (a dark story of ruthlessness and murder, Gothic horror, and three-way incest) as illustrative of Faulkner's achievements as a tragedian; others have found it self-obsessed and thus self-defeating or too dependent on remembrance of the resolution posed six years earlier in *The Sound and the Fury*. R. M. Adams selects the latter novel as a paradigm of his notion of open form, which is dedicated to the service of the tragic spirit[5]—and it is a tale told by an idiot, a death-enamored suicide, and a violent lost soul. *Sanctuary*, the "temple" of which is rudely violated, was eventually provided with a sequel (*Requiem for a Nun*) that some think is as mawkishly unconvincing in its salvationism as *Sanctuary* was gratuitously the popular shocker. *Light in August* tries to balance the Fascist crucifixion of Joe Christmas to glut a sadistic coldheartedness, with the Nativity story of Lena and Byron Bunch; but rather than meshing with one another, the stories seem juxtaposed, paratactic, mutually exclusive alternatives. *A Fable*, perhaps Faulkner's last attempt to so memorize another Golgotha as to uplift men's hearts for his own benefit, may some day find its successful apologist, but so far it seems to demonstrate the harpy at its most capricious and protean. For my purposes, these attempts at undiluted tragedy will make useful reference points, but will not be central exhibits; we shall try to perceive what I think is Faulkner's more congenital and congenial tragic vision, which is a mixed one.

A few years ago in *The New Yorker* Anthony West made a point in reviewing Alan Sillitoe's *Saturday Night and Sunday Morning* which may be helpful here.[6] He praises Sillitoe for having achieved a unique point of view for the novel, namely that "a realistic picture of existence can also be a cheerful one, and that no compromise or dishonesty is required to make it so." In general, the literature of the past, and particularly of the nineteenth century, he says, has a vision of the lower classes as in a state of continual moral and physical degradation, living in the "spirit-breaking machines" which are slums—both urban and rural. West calls attention to "the sap and vitality of the lower classes, which enable them not only to endure their abasement but to extract a great deal of pleasure and delight out of life." He believes that working-class life can be treated as "a normal aspect of the human condition," that people who live in a slum "happen to have been born there and not elsewhere," so "it does not represent the worst or even anything to be afraid of. . . . The universal choice is whether to be cruel and self-seeking or kind and generous, and it presents itself in a slum as it does anywhere else." He postulates the vigor and robust quality of popular songs and ballads and says that Sillitoe knows (like the songs) that there is a much worse fate than being born in a slum—not being born at all. This novel and the songs have a mutual quality of indomitability; they share the knowledge that "there are some joys which no measure of hardship can destroy and that, no matter what, life is worth living." This important truth about the human condition, he says, is one that literature (up to now) largely ignores.[7]

Noting several of Faulkner's favorite words in West's review—endured, indomitability, courage, the human condition—I would pursue some of the implications of his phrase, "life is worth living." It verges perilously on soap opera; and therein lies the danger of this whole approach—of *using* the dark and potentially tragic aspects of life in a meretricious way to jerk tears and set up a cheap, pat cheerfulness at the end. The opposite assertion, "Not to be born is the best for man," while certifiably tragic in being found in a choral ode of *Oedipus Coloneus*, is really one of the more outrageous grimaces of the demon, and a self-defeating one too. But the danger of both extremes can be avoided, and when it is successfully done, one gets what comes fairly close to a true balance and focus on the shifting comedy-tragedy spectrum.[8]

The broad background is laid in Faulkner's stories and novelettes —those regular and almost ritual, seasonal returns of his to the little people of his cosmos, the denizens of the country round about Jefferson: Varner's Crossroads, Frenchman's Bend, Sutpen's Hundred, Compson's Mile; the locale of *The Hamlet, Go Down Moses, As I Lay Dying, The Town, The Mansion.* The big "tragic" works are about the doomed and damned social elite, the faded or fading Southern aristocracy—Compsons, Sartorises, Carrotherses, Coldfields; the later "emergent" vision has as its heroes the descendants of these archetypes, who have survived the debacle and who take up the burden of responsibility in modern times: Gavin Stevens and Charles Mallison; Ike McCaslin; the later Temple Drake, perhaps; old Miss Habersham. And both these other visions have as their curse and their guilt and their conscience—Greeklike Furies and Fates—the solid, seemingly inert but irresistibly forceful mass, like the flywheel of a gyroscope, which are Faulkner's Negroes: Dilsey, Nancy, Joe Christmas; Luster; Aleck Sander; Lucas Beauchamp. All these have a glamor of some kind—that special ingredient which can (when successful) provide tragedy's inimitable lift and which can when unsuccessful plunge premature attempts at tragedy into bathos. I think Faulkner succeeds, in the big attempts and even more so in the "emergent" ones, as often perhaps as not and would suggest that this achievement is to no small degree due to his broad training in, and his instinctive return to for refreshment by, the outrageously comic vision of the human condition provided by his *un*glamorous Southerners: the rednecks, the poor whites, the sharecroppers and tenant farmers, the itinerant sewing-machine salesman (who is their chorus), and, unexpectedly perhaps, the very Snopses themselves, the carpetbaggers, the bollweevils of the post-war South.

For, to quote another American tragic writer, who also produced story-cycles as well as tragic epics—whose lightning-rod salesman may have been the prototype of Faulkner's sewing-machine man—Herman Melville: "Stubb has his history." And so do Cash Bundren and Henry Armstid and Vernon Tull and Jody Varner and Ratliff and Ek Snopes. And their histories—stories, tales—fit into the curve of tragedy (the dream, the fact, the confrontation, the acquiescence) rather as the lining, a homely but mitigating leather undergarment, fits the stiff and spiky bends of a heroic suit of armor. The first part of *The Hamlet* deals with the descent of Flem Snopes (like a fish-eyed Aeneas fleeing his Troy and on the make of an empire at the expense of any local Carthaginians or Latians)[9] upon Frenchman's Bend, the domain of Major de Spain and Uncle

Will Varner and his heir apparent, Jody. The stakes in this struggle, while not glamorous—and not invoking the transcendental, romantic sins and curses and dooms of Deep Tragedy—are still the basic ones of survival and aspiration, dreams of innocence and facts of guilt. In order for the Snopses to live and thrive, someone else has to suffer and lose. It is the struggle, first, for mere existence in a waste land (the reconstruction South), and then for advancement, for status, which is a fire gnawing at the vitals of even the meanest of men. Thoreau said, apropos of the little people of the world, that most men live lives of quiet desperation; this is certainly a tragic insight, but an incomplete one. Faulkner lifts it into the exhilarating realm of the tragic by evoking the demonic, by animating the desperation, and eminently by his transferral of the big words of tragic response to his homely, cheesy situations. There are gestures of defiance; acts of violence; Homeric battles of wit and epic trickeries—but all leavened and kept from the characteristically modern pitfall of bathos by turning the ludicrous into an asset instead of a danger: tears and laughter alternating and consuming one another.

Ab Snopes (Anchises to Flem's Aeneas, with overtones of Oedipus? he has a club foot) arrives to rent a farm from Jody Varner, with a legend already preceding him: his last contract had been with Major de Spain, and their struggle had been desperate indeed. In "outrage" (a favorite word here: Faulkner's vitalized version of quiet desperation) at what he considered the indignity done him by de Spain's meanness—the farmhouse "likely ain't fitten for hawgs"—he went up to the big house and, before going in the front door and walking on the hundred-dollar rug, deliberately stepped in a smoking pile of horse manure out in the driveway. De Spain made him clean the rug—and he had his womenfolks almost clean it to pieces with lye and brickbats. De Spain announced that Ab would have to pay for it by giving up twenty bushels of corn that "ain't even planted yet"; Ab countered by the outrageous action of *suing* de Spain before the justice of the peace, who cut down the outrageous mulct from twenty to ten bushels; and that night Ab (and his boy Flem) calmly set fire to de Spain's barn, watched it burn to the ground, and left the next day announcing, like a conquering warrior above the law, that he had cancelled his contract. I said this was the legend before him when he came to Varner's, and it gets some of its legendary (and thus potentially comitragic) quality from being related—told, acted— by Ratliff the sewing-machine man to Jody Varner, the elected next victim.

The upshot is that not only does Ab get the better of Jody on the farm but also Flem, the real founding father of the clan, the real genius of Snopesism, starts in as a clerk in Jody's store and succeeds, many sagas later, in marrying Eula Varner, the goddess-priestess of the whole county, and displacing all the local rulers by epic trickery and Odysseus-like daring. The last we see of him at this point, *he* is sitting in old Will Varner's barrel chair, on the front lawn of the symbolic old ruined Frenchman Place. It is a success story, the opposite of tragedy, so far, in strict terms; but he has had to cope all along with the forces of potential tragedy, and he has had his history. And the Varners and the villagers have struggled desperately and with outrage and horror and dismay in their hearts; they have had to relinquish their dreams and come to a humorously bitter, tears-and-laughter acquiescence in their defeat. And the tragic analogue that Faulkner discovered, or invented, about his cycle is that Flem Snopes's doom, though balked for now, is just put off, not evaded. Eula Varner, whom he finally possesses (or is possessed by) is really Hecate, or merciless Aphrodite, Helen the Destroyer: when she was at school, the monk-like master (whom she also destroyed) saw

a face eight years old and a body of fourteen with the female shape of twenty, which on the instant of crossing the threshold brought into the bleak, ill-lighted, poorly-heated room dedicated to the harsh functioning of Protestant primary education a moist blast of spring's liquorish corruption, a pagan triumphal prostration before the supreme primal uterus.

And although the troll has gone back under the bridge, it will emerge with authority and terror when it is time for Flem to meet his murderer, at the point of his greatest eminence and security.

Or take Henry Armstid and the other horseflesh-infatuated men of the story *Spotted Horses*—in its atmospherics one of the most hilarious of tall tales.[10] Flem Snopes (keeping in the background of course) arranges for a Texas man to bring to the hamlet a string of wild calico ponies and sell them to the dirt-poor local sharecroppers and villagers. They are critters out of this world, as they stand

> in a restive clump, larger than rabbits and gaudy as parrots and shackled to one another and to the wagon itself with sections of barbed wire, calico-coated, small bodied, with delicate legs and pink faces in which their mismatched eyes rolled wild and subdued, they huddled, gaudy, motionless and alert, wild as deer, deadly as rattlesnakes, quiet as doves.

These are exotic animals, bringing to the humdrum of village existence a whiff of magic—even if, as indeed it turns out, it is black magic and these are brimstone-fed incarnations of the demon world: "transmogrified hallucinations of Job and Jezebel," as even the Texas man calls them. They are Temptation: the very same two-faced goddess Peitho who haunts the *Oresteia*. For to these people, the vision of evil is marginality; their dream of innocence is a fling, a plunge, at whatever cost, into a more abundant life—to have something, just once, which is extra, a luxury, beyond the bare minimum for survival. Here is their chance; and they are just as infatuated by it as was Faustus with his dream of knowledge or Tamburlaine with his dream of glory.

Henry Armstid has led a life of quiet desperation, if anyone ever has. He can just barely keep himself and his family alive: he has never had a single gaudy thing of his own. As his wife, a gaunt, shapeless Jocasta or Job's wife, points out, "we got chaps in the house that never had shoes last winter. We ain't got corn to feed the stock. We got five dollars I earned weaving by firelight after dark. And he ain't no more despair than to buy one of them things." Henry Armstid just has to plunge once, hypnotized and goaded into classic folly and hubris by the outrageous, balefully attractive beasts. When Mrs. Armstid tries to stop him, he turns upon her "with that curious air of leashed, of dreamlike fury."

Several of the men, including Henry, buy the horses, and the Texas man and Flem leave. The men decide to catch up their horses; this is what happens:

The line was still advancing. The ponies milled, clotting, forced gradually backward toward the open door of the barn. Henry was still slightly in front, crouched slightly, his thin figure, even in the mazy moonlight, emanating something of that spent fury. The splotchy huddle of animals seemed to be moving before the advancing line of men like a snowball which they might have been pushing before them by some invisible means, gradually nearer and nearer to the black yawn of the barn door. Later it was obvious that the ponies were so intent upon the men that they did not realize the barn was even behind them until they backed into the shadow of it. Then an indescribable sound, a movement desperate and despairing, arose among them; for an instant of static horror men and animals faced one another, then the men whirled and ran before a gaudy vomit of long wild faces and splotched chests which overtook and scattered them and flung them sprawling aside and completely obliterated from sight Henry and the little boy. . . . They saw the horse the Texan had given them whirl and dash back and rush through the gate into Mrs. Littlejohn's yard and run up the front steps and crash once on the wooden veranda and vanish through the front door. Ek and the boy ran up onto the veranda. A lamp sat on a table just inside the door. In its mellow light they saw the horse fill the long hallway like a pinwheel, gaudy, furious, and thunderous. A little further down the hall there was a varnished yellow melodeon. The horse crashed into it; it produced a single note, almost a chord, in bass, resonant and grave, of deeply sober astonishment; the horse with its monstrous and antic shadow whirled again and vanished through another door. . . . It whirled again and rushed on down the hall and onto the back porch just as Mrs. Littlejohn, carrying an armful of clothes from the line and the washboard, mounted the steps. "Get out of here, you son of a bitch," she said. She struck and the horse whirled and rushed back up the hall, where Ek and the boy now stood. . . . The horse whirled without breaking or pausing. It galloped to the end of the veranda and took the railing and soared outward, hobgoblin and floating, in the moon. It landed in the lot still running and crossed the lot and galloped through the wrecked gate and among the overturned wagons and the still intact one in which Henry's wife still sat, and on down the lane and into the road.

Henry is trampled and hoof-beaten almost to death; the infatuated men spend the night chasing the devil-ponies all over the county, and one aspect of the outrageous comedy is the picture of Vernon Tull and his womenfolk meeting and having their wagon leaped into, on a bridge, by one of the same spotted varmints.[11] But, there is the acquiescence too; or at least, the endurance. The dogged Mrs. Armstid, still trying to get her five dollars back from Flem Snopes, has to undergo and accept the humiliation of his having cheated her husband, and the pathetic gift of a nickel's worth of striped candy—"a little sweetning for the chaps"—while her and Henry's world and year lie in ruins around them.

At the trial for damages, Mrs. Cora Tull (the God-fearing, Clytemnestra type of strong woman of *As I Lay Dying*), who starts off her agon "cold, furious, and contemptuous," looking for her "just rights and a punishment," is reduced to a dangerously comitragic condition of "calm and quiet":

> My team is made to run away by a wild spotted mad dog, my wagon is wrecked; my husband is jerked out of it and knocked unconscious and unable to work for a whole week with less than half of our seed in the ground, and I get nothing.

But it is worse than that: the Law, the instrument of inscrutable justice, decides that "now the horse that made your team run away and snatch your husband out of the wagon, belongs to you and Mr. Tull." She explodes one final time, screaming, shouting, almost as though she were really in possession of (or possessed by) the demon, before subsiding back into her wagon. And the raucous, hilarious Spirit Ironical brings the farce to a close with this court trial (a parody, in some respects, of the trial in Aeschylus's *Eumenides*) that demonstrates the inability of law to cope with the mysteriousness and the fearsome forces of life. "I can't stand no more!" the old Justice cried. "I won't! This court's adjourned! Adjourned!" This has affinities with that condition of exhaustion, or catharsis, at which tragedy arrives.

In this connection, we might mention briefly *As I Lay Dying*, an intricately counterpointed example of Faulkner's art in modulating the fact of death and man's dream of somehow ameliorating it or answering it. Here again the little, desperate people wage their unbelievable battle against indignity, and their frustrations and defeats are no less harrowing because they are ludicrous. While these are despised people, they are not despicable, and they are plagued by the same forces as confront the most glamorous tragic heroes: seduction, treachery, the unwanted life-force, and the temptation to abortion and murder; fire, flood, and the hard earth; lameness, madness, delusion, infatuation, desperation; the moral evils of hypocrisy and cupidity; the inevitable putrefaction of the flesh. Addie Bundren wanted to be buried in Jefferson, and, after a week of nightmare struggle, they get her there. Death has been paid its proper due; human beings have been equal to its occasion.

We pass on now to what I have called Faulkner's emergent works: his closest, I think, coming to terms with his tragic vision. The attempts at full tragedy are tours de force, virtuoso exercises in the murky depths; the comic stories are really too marvelously amusing to be "taken seriously." But Faulkner at least twice worked out, in the scope and detail worthy of the theme, a compromise version—one in which he tries to do justice both to his sense that the human condition *is* tragic and to his deeply-felt conviction that the human spirit can not only endure but prevail. And it is here that the Nay-saying spirit will be seen to emerge simultaneously with the everlasting Yea and assert its power and sovereignty.

Faulkner's progress, in one formulation, was "from photographic realism . . . to elevated realism . . . and then finally to myth."[12] And it is in the mythical realm that he works out his expiatory scheme, in the long story *The Bear*, combining the tragic myth of the Old South and its downfall with the more archetypal situation of man confronted by Nature, the wilderness, and invited or forced to learn to be a man, or how to be, in its image. (This is overplot, which has provided an anthropological matrix for tragedy from the beginnings.) The enveloping story[13] of the hunt for Old Ben, the bear, takes on all the qualities of the proto-religious initiation rites and ceremonies: to be a good hunter one must be also a pure and willing victim (the hero's name is Isaac, and Faulkner makes much of the Old Testament parallel); one must "shed or expiate the guilt accumulated in society." Ike McCaslin undergoes his training, his probation, and his initiation, as he participates in "the yearly pageant-rite of the old bear's furious immortality." He must learn to be humble and enduring, or the wilderness-Nature will not show herself to him; and the method of becoming worthy is one of the central tropes of tragedy: renunciation, relinquishment. Faulkner plays a variation on this concept, in the bear story: we are accustomed to the hard tragic lesson learned by, say, King Lear, that his brusque and proud repudiation of his crown must turn into a total renunciation of earthly values before he is ready to crawl towards death; in the hunt part of Faulkner's story Ike McCaslin learns that he must relinquish *to* the wilderness, give up successively his guide, his gun, his watch, and his compass—those tools and symbols of man's arrogant control over nature—before he is granted the almost sacramental epiphany, the manifestation of the goddess.

There are several dimensions of overplot: the seasonal, primordial rhythm of life and death and rebirth, in Nature and in the spirit of man; the ordeal of a whole people, the South, to get free from the curse inherently entangled in its destiny; the dimension of the time machine, Faulkner's device of the chronicle (which is incorporated in the ledgers of the McCaslin clan, "the yellowed pages in their fading and implacable succession," that Ike has to relive, reenact, by reading through and accepting as his own family history—and which Faulkner explicitly compares to The Book itself, the Old Testament); and the sudden soaring into the rarefied air of Truth and its complexity, on the one hand, and of the mystery of God and creation and that piety for his creation that even God is afflicted by, on the other. All these overplots, or extra dimensions of tragic meaning, merge with and complement each other, as well as reflect and spring from the central human action of the story. For example, we are told that Ike finally won his quasi-priestly manhood and acquiesced in what that meant he must give up: "Still the woods would be his mistress and his wife." *His* wilderness (even while the physical trees were being cut down in the name of progress) "soared, musing, inattentive, myriad, eternal, green. The woods did not change, and timeless, would not."

> Because there was no death, not Lion and not Sam: not held fast in earth, myriad yet undiffused of every myriad part, leaf and twig and particle, air and sun and rain and dew and night, acorn oak and leaf and acorn again, dark and dawn and dark and dawn again in their immutable progression, and being myriad, one; and Old Ben too.

Then at one point in their long discussion, Ike and his cousin get to talking about truth and how one can manage to know it: statements are made like "there is only one truth and it covers all things that touch the heart" and men can "comprehend truth only through the complexity of passion and lust and hate and fear which drives the heart"—"they all touch the heart, and what the heart holds to becomes truth as far as we know truth." This eminently Pascalian idea is a bit hard to take, in the abstract, and Edmonds reaches down a volume of poetry:

> "Listen," he said. He read the five stanzas aloud and closed the book on his finger and looked up. "All right," he said. "Listen," and read again, but only one stanza this time and closed the book and laid it on the table. "She cannot fade, though thou hast not thy bliss," McCaslin said: "Forever wilt thou love, and she be fair."

"He's talking about a girl," he said.

"He had to talk about something," McCaslin said. Then he said, "He was talking about truth. Truth is one. It doesn't change. It covers all those things which touch the heart—honor and pride and pity and justice and courage and love. Do you see now?" He didn't know. Somehow it had seemed simpler than that. . . .

But saying No to death has always needed the deceptively simple complexities of poetry. To match his own seasonal return to homely analogues of myth, Faulkner displays this strong affinity for the Wordsworthian lyric statement—not held fast in earth but free in earth; rolled round with rocks and stones and trees—and the Keatsian sublime.[14]

Or another sudden coalescing of intimations of immanence and transcendence: they are going over the old ledgers, the bloody and foolish and cursed story of the South; and fugitive analogies to the bloody and foolish and cursed history of the Chosen People in the Old Testament keep coming to the surface, until *He* suddenly appears as central to the story's meaning.

because He had seen how in individual cases they were capable of anything, any height or depth remembered in mazed comprehension out of heaven where hell was created too, and so He must admit them or else admit his equal somewhere and so be no longer God and therefore must accept responsibility for what He himself had done in order to live with Himself in His lonely and paramount heaven. . . .

Until one day He said . . . *This is enough* . . . and He could have repudiated them since they were his creation now and forever more throughout all their generations, until not only that old world from which He had rescued them but this new one too which He had revealed and led them to as a sanctuary and refuge were become the same worthless tideless rock cooling in the last crimson evening, except that

one man, John Brown (like Noah?), was found faithful and strong, and the women *at least*[15] succored the sick and hungry; so He arranged the Civil War as a tragic way to bring His people to their senses—He "who had made them and could know no more of grief than He could of pride or hope: *Apparently they can learn nothing save through suffering, remember nothing save when underlined in blood.*" It is not hard-core tragedy, of course; we are dangerously near again to the willful salvationalism of "Nothing can be whole. . . ." But the tough tragic strengths are there—"nothing save when."

On the side of form, we get one more indication that the tragic aspects of *The Bear* are appropriately modern—that is, partial, a bit wistful, made available only fitfully and to a few and to those few only personally and precariously. There are characteristically two plots, two tropes, in Ike's try for a solution to his dilemma: first, the attempt (like Raskolnikov's, like Lord Jim's) to expiate it, to pay off the debt, to repudiate the accumulated burden of his history; this is his dream of innocence, of acquittal. He tries it by reliving the chronicle, making the actual journey-quest to pay the money debt, giving up ownership of the land, and so on; but this is not decisive even for the individual act of freedom. The other trope, the stylized, formal, ritual ordination (in its enveloping action), has come closer to setting him free. Yet this container too —the assertion of a sacramental value system in which godlike power and action are codified into the virtues of the hunt under the banner of Honor—reveals its vulnerability even within its own terms. R. W. B. Lewis sets up the connection well:

> It is something composed of a cluster of virtues unambiguously present from the beginning . . . together they are what we may call the honorable: something Roman and a trifle stiff, but independent of the fluctuations of moral fashions in the city . . . a solid set of conventions and rules, faultlessly observed on both sides.[16]

But it is just such concepts—of honor and Romanness and solidity —that Shakespeare's critical inquiry teaches us to beware of: they are indeed ideal and godlike and establishmentarian, but they are far from unambiguous.[17]

The failure, even in the expanded version of *The Bear*, of Ike's assault upon the demon of selfishness—the acquiescence of his dream of innocence *as* innocence in recognition of its futility—has been documented from many points of view.[18] This is a good office of criticism, which makes the case against the too sanguine conclusions of the converted who leap to the much desired affirmation that the "miracle of moral regeneration," the transmutation, the transition, the transcendence, the transformation, have taken place; that the containment has been successful. And important testimony comes from Faulkner himself as an outside critic commenting adversely on his own hero: "I think a man ought to do more than just repudiate. He should have been more affirmative instead of shunning people."[19] But this kind of obiter dictum, in an interview setting, is necessarily superficial; the real recognition displays itself in *Delta Autumn*, sequel to *The Bear*[20] and severe critique of it. Faulkner is still writing the books, under the tutelage of the unpitying demon.

Ike McCaslin, having tried to compromise with renunciation by way of (selective) relinquishment, now finds himself confronted by the specter of repudiation and refusal. On the latter-day hunting trip into the Delta, all attempts to reconstitute the old magic are confronted by facts and symbols of failure. Roth (Carrothers) Edmonds—bearer of the bad old and the hopeful new names and titular head of the clan—shows up as careless and selfish, sullen and ruthless. Ike goes along to try to do for Roth what Sam Fathers had done for him, but fails, in a precisely tragic way. We can observe it best (as always) in the words, the poetry: three tropes carry the main burden of the tragic action.

The overplot theme of decline, deliquescence, inexorable decay is sounded at the outset: they "enter the Delta . . . the last hill, at the foot of which the rich unbroken alluvial flatness began as the sea began at the base of its cliffs, dissolving away beneath the unhurried November rain as the sea itself would dissolve away."[21] It returns periodically, accompanying each movement of the plot, undergoing delicate variations like "retreating," "retrograde," the "thin stain" of daylight "snared somewhere between the river's surface and the rain"; "the constant murmur of rain" gradually envelops the tent ("The motionless belly of rain-murmured canvas," "the rain-murmured canvas globe"), that shelter and would-be tabernacle of Ike's would-be sacrament. At the last, "the tent held only silence and the sound of rain. And cold too": the "faint light and the constant and grieving rain" preside; the tent is empty. We have observed Shakespeare's counterattack on the demon of erosion, in *Antony and Cleopatra*, and his coming to terms with it in *The Tempest;* it is an earnest of Faulkner's loyalty to the hard tragic that he envelops his admission of Ike's failure not in dynamic dissolution, but in rain as the universal solvent, constant in grief. The thing contained has become the container.

Ike's dream of innocence has been of peace, of relaxation, letting go. It was this that he had apparently achieved in the early episodes of *The Bear,* even though it had to be earned and came in a sudden, swooping rush. Now, as he proceeds through the agon against his grandnephew's reiterated "harshness" and "savagery" and "ruthlessness," he maintains for a while his ascendancy, "peaceful, without regret or fretting." Even at Roth's direct attack—"Where have you been all the time you were dead?"—he remains "*still* peaceful and untroubled and merely grave"; "even into the laughter," he spoke in "that peaceful and *still* untroubled voice." And (accompanied always by that ambivalent, ominous *still, yet, even*) he achieves peaceful sleep, lulled by his reveries and his self-justifications, until—"Something jarred sharply." Harshness breaks in, and now he must take the poison: it is the girl who, in their agon, regards him "almost peacefully," "with immersed contemplation," while he cries and springs and flings himself, "awry-haired, glaring"; he goes up to and through the paroxysm of harshness, to subside—"harshly, rapidly, but not so harsh now and soon not harsh at all but just rapid, urgent . . . his voice . . . running away with him and he had neither intended it nor could stop it"—while she looks "quietly" down at him. He had been able to fight off Roth's brutal accusation that he had learned nothing about how people really are; now, having transferred his armor of peacefulness to the girl and having accepted the guilt of harshness as his own, he has no answer to her devastating question, "Old Man, have you lived so long and forgotten so much that you don't remember anything you ever knew or felt or even heard about love?" He lies back—this time, "trembling, panting . . . rigid save for the shaking." One final flurry, with Legate "rummaging hurriedly among the still-tumbled blankets," makes him move "suddenly," only to lie back down, "his crossed hands once more weightless on his heart." His catharsis is a harsh and grieving peace.

The final, and decisive, acquiescence is in the reality and autonomy of the negative: the recognition of what is involved in the capacity of human beings to say No. Several times in *The Bear* Ike had tried with his *at least* to deny the totalitarian claims of death. He had even mobilized the last reserves ("No! No! . . . No, I tell you. I won't. I can't. Never") against his wife's demand that he take back the plantation—only to be confronted by a greater piety to the Dread Spirit, in the form of woman who, "listening to nothing, thinking of nothing . . . , looking at nothing . . . , waiting for nothing," pulled him down into her hell with "still the steady and invincible hand and he said Yes and he thought, *She is lost. She was born lost. We were all born lost.*" Now, in the reverie-interval of *Delta Autumn*, Faulkner chooses three things for Ike to remember: that day when he had been blooded by his first deer-kill plus its reenactment when he confronted McCaslin Edmonds; the scene of his capitulation to the woman, "himself and his wife juxtaposed in their turn against the same land"; and the strategy of saying No by going to the very bottom of his budget of minimums: "in repudiation and denial *at least* of the land and the wrong and shame *even if* he couldn't cure the wrong and eradicate the shame," "*at least* in principle, and *at least* the land itself in fact, for his son *at least*," "would *at least* save and free his son, *and* saving and freeing his son, lost him." He had lost the wife too, twice—"lost her, because she loved him."

Suddenly, it comes to him why he had not tried to apply his *at least* policy to salvaging his wilderness—because, by maintaining an exact ratio between himself and the wilderness he would be able to keep the equation eternally in the penultimate stage, the precarious balance, denying the final step to zero: "the two spans running out together, not towards oblivion, nothingness, but into a dimension free of both time and space," where immortal game would run forever before immortal hounds and fall to rise phoenix-like again and again. This is an exercise in heroic egoism comparable to Lord Jim's, and it is put into jeopardy, tragically, each November by Ike even though "he ain't got any business in the woods" any more. He achieves his initial victory—peaceful sleep—in these terms, but —"the tent-flap swung in and fell." Roth comes back and begins the massive injection of nothingness: "give the messenger this and tell—say I said No." " 'Tell her No,' he said. 'Tell her.' " "Nothing! . . . Nothing! This is all of it. Tell her I said No." There is a confrontation scene reminiscent of that between Jim and Gentleman Brown: Ike and Roth "stared at one another—the old face, wan, sleep-raddled above the tumbled bed, the dark and sullen younger one at once furious and cold." Ike must *tell* her what Roth had *said;* he too must maintain his piety to nothingness, to refusal, which involves the oblivion and repudiation of whatever he had known of love, because it was Ike himself who spoiled Roth, failed to make a man of him, when he selfishly gave up the land to Roth's grandfather.

The rest of it carries through in the grip of the new mode; Ike begins by acknowledging his kinship—"You're Uncle Isaac," she said. "Yes," he said—and then immediately moves over to the negative—"But never mind that. Here. Take it. He said to tell you No."—and keeps saying *No, not, didn't, don't, never mind.* He *lacks* his spectacles, can*not* complete the reach of his hand, *with-*

draws beneath the blanket, *ain't* got his pants on, and can*not* get up to put them on; "his voice was running away with him and he had neither intended it nor could stop it." The coda—the dream of relaxation and freedom and peace acquiescing (literally) into *lying back down*, hands crossed and weight*less* in the *empty* tent, into accepting the verdict of "nothing extra" amid the only constancy, that of the dissolving and grieving rain—modulates exquisitely to the dying fall. But, as with many, perhaps most, successful tragedies, the real death had come earlier, when he performed his last act of repudiation: "Then go. . . . Get out of here! I can do nothing for you! Can't nobody do nothing for you!" It is between the old Justice of *Spotted Horses* ("I can't stand no more! Adjourned!") and Lear's No, No; Never, Never; Nothing!—and it is closer to the deep finality, the general woe and great decay, of the latter. Periodically, it seems, Faulkner finds that he must give presence to the adversary, in spite of (or perhaps because of) his elaborately containing form.

Ike McCaslin was the last of his line: he had no surviving children. But Faulkner's world of characters are all one family and one another's keepers, and the torch passed on to another pair—uncle and nephew—Gavin Stevens and Chick Mallison, in *Intruder in the Dust*. Again we have the author as tragic hero: struggling with great pains and through frustrations and temptations and failures and partial perceptions toward the true and final form which his dream of innocence urges him to express; wrestling with the demon, struggling around Cape Horn, writing the books. Faulkner worked out his dream of Ike McCaslin's personal success and then found it too vulnerable to the facts of guilt; but, building on this partial perception, he starts the rhythm again, laying himself open to another possible defeat and disillusionment, but each time—this time, perhaps—getting a little further along.

It is in *Intruder* that one of Faulkner's most ringing and best known formulations of his salvationist tragic vision occurs: "But then the whole chronicle of man's immortality is in the suffering he has endured, his struggle toward the stars in the stepping-stones of his expiations." This is indeed a credal formula, verging perhaps on the frenetic with its hypnotic alliterativeness; but let us explicate a few of its implications to see whether it can be authenticated by the novel of which it might be thought of as an internal epigraph. *Expiation* is the key word; the OED spreads it out for us:

> expiate, *v.* 1594 [from L. *expiare*, to atone for fully, f. ex- + *piare* to propitiate, f. *pius*, devout.] 1. To avert by religious ceremonies, *Obs.* except *Antiq.* [and except such revivers of antique virtue as Faulkner?]—1611.2. To purify with religious rites—1660. 3. To extinguish the guilt of—1608. 4. To pay the penalty of—1665. 5. To make reparation for—1626. 6. To extinguish by suffering to the full; to end by death—1615.

Nobody among the main characters ends by death in *Intruder:* it is a "comedy." But, like the whole Faulknerian vision we have glimpsed, it is flirting with death all the way; one cannot say No except in the presence of the thing negated. Lucas Beauchamp is in imminent danger of being immolated—lynched and burned up in gasoline—during the whole action; three men do meet violent ends: one shot in the back, another's head bashed in with a shovel, the third a suicide; and the central act is as morbid an ordeal as ever confronted a candidate for manhood, the compulsion to dig up a corpse at midnight. These things add incomparably to the urgency, the outrageousness, of the demand made on the hero; but it is in the real death, that of the spirit, that Faulkner's tragic insights inhere. Chick Mallison, spiritual heir of Ike McCaslin, having been fatefully elected for his role by his baptism in the icy creek one December day; having had his callow dream of innocence, of maintaining the status quo of white Southern supremacy, unforgettably confronted by the recalcitrant, the intractable, fact of Lucas Beauchamp's stubbornness and refusal to act like a nigger; desiring passionately either to escape his involvement or to brazen it out like his fellow white men—Chick responds to the mute demand, overcomes his fears and his repugnancies and his outrage, and, with his "brother" Aleck Sander and old Miss Habersham (the thinkers, like his Uncle Gavin, and the doers, the menfolks of the South, being stymied from action, it is up to the "womens and the children"), acts and endures and succeeds. But his vindication is bitter, in the tragic way, because for him to be right means that his fellow-townsmen and neighbors and kinsmen have to be acknowledged as wrong and pusillanimous and unjust and selfish and cowardly and unmanly. This is the endlessly fascinating aspect of tragedy: it is homogeneous; it feeds on its own poison, bites its own tail. For Chick to become a man (at sixteen, as had Ike) he must renounce, give up, relinquish his childish ideal of manliness; in asserting and proving his own manhood he must acknowledge the emasculation of his peers: they behave like a faceless mob.

But he goes through with it and learns by it, and he keeps the flame alive. Chick Mallison is the hero of this story, and we see it all through his eyes and his developing consciousness. We undergo, with him, the powerful rhythms of tragedy; but what makes this the high-water mark, perhaps, of Faulkner's movement is that here for the first time the main actor and sufferer is buttressed, on both sides, by major aides. One is Lucas Beauchamp—the only one of Faulkner's Negroes who really deserves the epithets *indomitable* and *intractable* as well as the relatively pale *enduring:* he is conscience aroused and come to life; he dominates the action, and he has the last word. This is something more than Dilsey and Joe Christmas. The other is Gavin Stevens, a reincarnation of Mr. Compson and Hightower and McCaslin Edmonds, but this time a workable and working and teachable reason, an ethical power, "at least" not impotent, but capable of being brought to bear on that which the hero sees intuitively and acts manfully. Faulkner is no longer thwarted by the failure or breakdown of his forces: they stand up all the way; they go the distance; they take the tension and strain of the tragic curve. It is an exciting and exhilarating performance.

After the attempt at Christian-fabulous theodicy in *A Fable,*

Faulkner, still struggling with the option that the tricky gods present him and his hero, returned at the end, in *The Rievers*, to his middle vision and statement—comic-tragic, partially yet outrageously romantic. And, gratuitously, almost as a reward for our own struggles with this uncanny demon, our phrase from Shakespeare turns up, and in the same quizzical, chancy way it came to Autolycus in *The Winter's Tale:*

> Who serves Virtue works alone, unaided, in a chilly vacuum of reserved judgment; where, pledge yourself to Non-Virtue and the whole countryside boils with volunteers to help you. . . . It was as if *the gods themselves* had offered him these scot-free hours between eleven-two and sunset, he to scorn, ignore them at his peril.

But *The Rievers* is not, any more than *Intruder in the Dust* is, a tragedy in anything like the full sense; and this brings us full circle to the end of our exploration. It is not a tragedy because it has lost sight of the overplot—there are almost no metaphysical reverberations, and the highest idealism glimpsed is a sort of partial humanism—and because they are success stories: the acquiescence in defeat is not required of the hero. "Don't stop," Uncle Gavin tells Chick; you did it once, and you can do it again, and you have shown others how it can be done.

"I decline," said Faulkner in the Nobel Prize acceptance speech, "to accept the end of man." "Man will not merely endure: he will prevail." It is a noble and inspiriting remark that is all the more heartening because it is said by one who has earned, the hard way, the right to say it. And maybe he is right.[22] But if he is, it will be in spite of his long and complex "affair with tragedy," not because of it; or because of it to the degree that he has not avoided it, but used it and overcome it by sheer will power. The protean tragic daemon has met its match in Faulkner's inexhaustible ability to spin an enveloping cocoon, an indefinitely expansible, as well as self-regenerating, container. But the container would never have been woven, or even conceived, were it not for the ineradicable knowledge, and acknowledgement, of the thing itself.

Notes

PREFACE

1. Norman O. Brown, *Love's Body*, New York, Random House, 1966, pp. 188, 247, 190.
2. Noted from J. Hillis Miller, *Poets of Reality*, Cambridge, Mass., Harvard Univ. Press, 1965, p. 242. "This means," Miller comments, "that the images of a poem cannot be voluntarily controlled. They just happen."
3. John Barth, *The Floating Opera*, New York, Avon Books, 1956, pp. 263–64.

I. ASPECTS OF TRAGEDY: FORM AND FEATURE

1. Friedrich Nietzsche, *The Birth of Tragedy* and *The Genealogy of Morals* (trans. F. Golffing), Garden City, N. Y., Doubleday, 1956, p. 130; G. Wilson Knight, *The Wheel of Fire*, London, Methuen, 1930, p. xx; W. H. Auden, "Under Which Lyre," Phi Beta Kappa Poem, Harvard, 1946—*Nones*, London, Faber and Faber, 1946.
2. *The Faerie Queene*, I.IV.iv–v.
3. Ibid.

4. Ibid., I.IX.xliii.1–6.

5. Ibid., I.X.lx.7–9.

6. Ibid., IV.IV.xli8–9.

7. Letter to Ralegh.

8. Wordsworth, *The Prelude* (1805), Bk. I, ll. 230–31.

9. Frederick J. Pottle ("Wordsworth and Freud, or the Theology of the Unconscious," *Bulletin of the General Theological Seminary* for June 1948, Chelsea Square, New York, pp. 1–12) finds that Wordsworth's vision from Mount Snowdon is a "great consoling figure of the human mind" (p. 10) and that Wordsworth was right in "his intuition that God dwells in the unconscious mind . . . it is His territory and not that of the Potentates of the dark Present." Any other view, he suggests, would "commit us to that Gnostic or Manichaean dualism which Christianity firmly repudiated at its very beginning." But there's the rub: how can we—how did Wordsworth—avoid such a commitment?

10. *The Rape of Lucrece*, ll. 1365–1582.

11. Ibid.

12. *A Midsummer Night's Dream*, V.i.5–6, 19–20.

13. Murray Krieger, *A Window to Criticism: Shakespeare's Sonnets and Modern Poetics*, Princeton, N. J., Princeton Univ. Press, 1964.

14. *Birth of Tragedy*, p. 52.

15. R. P. Blackmur, "The Loose and Baggy Monsters of Henry James: Notes on the Underlying Classic Form in the Novel," *Accent*, Summer 1951, 129–46; p. 129.

16. Lucius W. Elder, *A Criticism of Some Attempts to Rationalize Tragedy* [University of Pennsylvania Ph.D. Thesis, 1915 (?)] This remarkable work, the voice of one crying in the wilderness fifty years before his time, eminently deserves real publication and wide dissemination. Elder put a probing finger on the rationalist fallacies of all the enlightenments, and struck out many anticipations of middle-twentieth-century insights into our subject. See note 30 for chapter 1.

17. *All's Well*, II.iii.1–7.

18. Murray Krieger, *The Tragic Vision*, New York, Holt, Rinehart & Winston, 1960, p. 3.

19. Nietzsche too, for all his penetrating insight into these basic antinomies, cannot quite keep them from overlapping and merging (so strong, perhaps, was his own emotional and artistic drive toward synthesis). Here are a few exemplary texts (from *The Birth of Tragedy*):

[the Hamlet-hero is inhibited from action by] not reflection but understanding, the apprehension of truth and its terror . . . nausea invades him. (pp. 51–52)

Then, in this supreme jeopardy of the will, art, that sorceress expert in healing, approaches; only she can turn his fits of nausea into imaginations with which it is possible to live. . . . the threatening paroxysms I have mentioned were contained by the intermediary of those Dionysiac attendants. (p. 52)

In his transformation he [the Dionysiac reveller] sees a new vision, which is the Apollonian completion of his state. And by the same token this new vision completes the dramatic act. (p. 56)

Tragedy is an Apollonian embodiment of Dionysiac insights and powers, and for that reason separated by a tremendous gulf from the epic. (pp. 56–57)

20. E. T. Owen, *The Harmony of Aeschylus*, Toronto, Clark, Irwin, 1952, p. 27; George Steiner, *The Death of Tragedy*, New York, Hill and Wang, 1961, p. 79.

21. Francis Ferguson, *The Idea of a Theatre*, Princeton, N. J., Princeton Univ. Press, 1949, p. 18.

22. After this was written I encountered Karl S. Guthke's *Modern Tragicomedy—An Investigation into the Nature of the Genre* (New York, Random House, 1966), in which he summarizes very usefully the theories of modern students of literary genre, notably the idea of "inner form," "an underlying general attitude towards reality, a mode of confronting life in general." He thus expands Karl Vietor's *Vermutungs- und Ahnungsbild* (a tentative and intuitive image): "This intuitive idea may lead us to the identification and appreciation of other tragicomedies and, as it does so, it is further corrected, expanded, modified, refined, and validated. And vice versa. . . ." (pp. 92–93). Practically all, however, of Guthke's admirable efforts toward a definition lead him into what I find to be a tacit admission that tragicomedy is not really a genre of itself, but shares the hard core of tragedy: what he arrives at should perhaps be called at most comitragedy.

23. Its derivation, and an explication of its five terms, were first set forth in my article, "The Possibility of a Christian Tragedy" (*Thought*, XXXI, 1956, 403–28; reprinted in *Tragedy: Modern Essays in Criticism*, ed. Michel and Sewall, Englewood Cliffs, N. J., Prentice-Hall, 1963,

210–33). Other explorations of its validity and usefulness may be found in my "Shakespearean Tragic Poetry: Critique of Humanism from the Inside" (*Massachusetts Review*, II, 1961, 633–50) and "Hamlet: Superman, SubChristian" (*Centennial Review*, VI, 1962, 230–44).

The elements of the formula received (somewhere along the line) a corroboration from Freud's dictum:

> die ersten und ursprünglichen Entstehen direkt bei dem Zusammentreffen des Ichs mit einem übergrossen Libidoansprüch aus traumatischen Momenten, sie bilden ihre Angst neu. . . .

which proved susceptible, in one translation, of my kind of formulaic expression: "A trauma is constituted when the ego comes into contact with an excessive demand of its own libido." (*Neue Folge der Vorlesungen zur Einfürung in die Psychoanalyse*, Gesammelte Werke, London, Imago, 1940, vol. 15, p. 101.

For purposes of comparison, here are several other efforts at formulation undertaken in recent works devoted to our subject:

> A work of art is tragic if it substantiates the following situation: *A protagonist who commands our earnest good will is impelled in a given world by a purpose, or undertakes an action, of a certain seriousness and magnitude; and by that very purpose or action, subject to that same given world, necessarily and inevitably meets with grave spiritual or physical suffering.* (Oscar Mandel, *A Definition of Tragedy*, New York, New York Univ. Press, 1961, p. 20.)

> Tragedy is (1) a form of a literature that (2) presents a symbolic action as performed by actors and (3) moves into the center immense human suffering, (4) in such a way that it brings to our minds our own forgotten and repressed sorrows as well as those of our kin and humanity, (5) releasing us with some sense (a) that suffering is universal—not a mere accident in our experience, (b) that courage and endurance in suffering or nobility in despair are admirable—not ridiculous—and usually also (c) that fates worse than our own can be experienced as exhilarating. (6) In length, performances range from a little under two hours to about four, and the experience is highly concentrated. (Walter Kaufmann, *Tragedy and Philosophy*, Garden City, N. Y., Doubleday & Company, 1968, p. 85.)

> *A tragedy is a final and impressive disaster due to an unforeseen or unrealized failure involving people who command respect and sympathy. It often entails an ironical change of fortune and usually con-*

veys a strong impression of waste. It is always accompanied by misery and emotional distress. (Geoffrey Brereton, *Principles of Tragedy*, Coral Gables, Fla., University of Miami Press, 1968, p. 20.)

Certain features of what Brereton calls "the legacy of Aristotle," notably the involvement of the spectator and identification with an art-form, have proved ineradicable from these substantive, stipulative, general "definitions," and they sooner or later undermine or render inconsistent the arguments of each of these valuable books. (The latter two, Kaufmann's and Brereton's, reached me when this book was in the copy-editing stage, and I have not attempted to either enlist their support for my views or document my points of disagreement. Both are too wide-ranging and deep-probing to be done justice to by epitomizing; they will surely have to be coped with by any student of the subject.)

24. Pierre Teilhard de Chardin, *The Phenomenon of Man*, (trans. Bernard Wall) New York, Harper and Row, 1959, pp. 29, 56, 50, 51, 57, *passim*, 309.

The physicists too are subject to the dry mock of the cartoonist: see Alan Dunn's white-on-black scene of a lecturer proposing to his ghostly interlocutors that, "Incredible as it may seem to those of us who live in the world of anti-matter, a mirror image exists—the reverse of our-selves—which we can only call the world of matter." (*The New Yorker*, July 7, 1965, p. 31).

Recently (*Cross Currents*, XVIII, 2, Spring 1968, 139) John J. Mc-Mahon has assessed Teilhard's Omega Point as "the most intellectually fruitful (i.e., the most illuminating for coordinating other data) and the most humanly motivating (i.e., the most capable of releasing human energies) hypothesis." But he proceeds to demonstrate that although this is Teilhard's appeal in our age, "It is also his Achilles' heel."

25. Alfred North Whitehead, *Adventures of Ideas*, New York, Macmillan, 1937, p. 381.

26. Robert Louis Stevenson, *Works*, London, Heinemann et al., 1922, XII, 291, 286, 292.

27. Cited from *Renaissance England* (ed. Roy Lamson and Hallett Smith), New York, Norton, 1942, pp. 517, 514.

28. T. S. Eliot, "The Hollow Men", *Collected Poems*, New York, Harcourt, Brace, 1930, p. 104.

29. Arthur Koestler, *The Yogi and the Commissar*, New York, Macmillan, 1946, p. 232.

30. Koestler, *Insight and Outlook*, New York, Macmillan, 1949; *The Age of Longing*, New York, Macmillan, 1951.
Compare Elder (*op. cit.*, note 16 above):

The destruction of everything local, the falsity of all particular truths, is the earnest of the reality of all Truth. . . . The death of the specific person liberates the new ideal from the limitations of a finite consciousness . . . only in that process can it find its proper worth and expression. (p. 25)

The inner movement and life of the absolute is the outer movement and death of the parts (cf. Bradley, *Appearance and Reality*, ch. xxvi). The burden of carrying on the work of the universe rests on the parts; hence the necessary expansion of the latter to meet new needs is supposed to be a usurpation by the parts of the function of the whole. . . . [19th century speculation said that] the world is real as a whole; its parts are only phenomena. Man as an individual is no less a transgressor against the divinity of the world than he was formerly thought to be a sinner against God's law by Adam's fall. (p. 54)

The individual is a member of many higher organizations; the higher the institution the more does it demand a proportionate negation of his purely personal or subjective nature. (p. 59)

31. Albert Camus, *The Myth of Sisyphus and Other Essays* (trans. Justin O'Brien), New York, Random House, pp. 21, 38, 91.
Camus is the central exhibit in Charles I. Glicksberg's *The Tragic Vision in 20th Century Literature* (Carbondale, Southern Illinois Univ. Press, 1963), in which two persistent claims of humanistic tragic theory are reasserted as characteristic and definitive: the hero's courage as revelatory of human greatness and the act of writing, of producing a work of art, as the achievement of tragic success. "Like Weil, Camus insists that all, without exception, must be saved." "Whatever the metaphysical foundation on which it rests, the tragic experience must affirm life and celebrate, as we have said, the greatness of the human spirit." Glicksberg quotes a splendidly resonant bit of early (1925) O'Neill:

I'm always acutely conscious of the Force behind (Fate, God, our biological past creating our present, whatever one calls it, Mystery certainly)—and of the one eternal tragedy of Man in his glorious, self-destructive struggle to make the Force express him instead of being, as an animal is, an infinitesimal incident in its expression. And my proud assertion is that this is the only subject worth writing about and that it is possible—or can be—to develop a tragic expression in terms of transfigured modern values and symbols in the theatre which may to some degree bring home to members of a modern audience their ennobling identity with the tragic figures on the stage. . . .

He cites this apparently without seeing the inference of its irrelevancy for tragic theory in the fact, as he notes later, that O'Neill in his last period—*The Iceman Cometh*—"returned to nihilism."

Glicksberg cites André Gorz on Sartre to the effect that the existentialist tragedian "invents this way out for himself: to write about the non-meaning of life . . . this demonstration itself, and the remedy it provides against the experience it contradicts." He claims that Gottfried Benn, "the nihilist par excellence, turns to art as his last defence"; and himself returns at the end to Camus: "After all, that is why I am an artist, because even the work that negates still affirms something and does homage to the wretched and magnificent life that is ours." But again, apparently without seeing the ironic implications, he had concluded the Camus chapter with this: "Camus died before he could fully develop his concept of tragedy. The myth of the absurd failed to give birth to the tragic hero. Unfortunately the potentialities for affirmation present in the literature of revolt were overshadowed by the myth of meaninglessness which lay like a blight upon the cultural landscape." Unfortunately, indeed, for the "myth of meaninglessness" underlay, like a demon, the Promethean, Apollonian, programmatic, assertive affirmation. Lionel Abel (*Metatheatre*, New York, Hill & Wang, 1963, p. 141) points out that Camus, *qua* high priest of "the absurd," is really non-sensical, and without adequate philosophical pretensions.

32. Cited from *The Portable Conrad* (ed. Morton D. Zabel), New York, Viking, 1949, pp. 15–16.

33. "1919"; *Autobiography*, Garden City, N. Y., Doubleday, 1958, pp. 128, 132, 138, 353; *Essays and Introductions*, London, Macmillan, 1961, pp. 109, 242, 245.

34. B. L. Reid, *W. B. Yeats: The Lyric of Tragedy*, Norman, Oklahoma Univ. Press, 1961, p. 214.

35. Thomas MacFarland's recent *Tragic Meanings in Shakespeare* (New York, Random House, 1966), while recognizing all the right

things, obdurately refuses to come to the conclusions about tragedy that are implied by his phenomenology. A superb reading of *Antony and Cleopatra* is marred by a failure to recognize that the play achieves its transcendent victory precisely because it goes beyond tragedy; his last pages on *Hamlet* (which acknowledge its ultimate vision as one of "universal night") belie all the antecedent apologia for its humanism, etc.; the chapter on *Othello* is almost so Bradleyan as to be embarrassing; and he cannot point out (most acutely) the process of "reduction" in Lear without giving equal time to the celebration of a "renewal" which has no more justification now than in the time and sensibility of Nahum Tate.

36. Cited from Vivienne Koch, *W. B. Yeats: The Tragic Phase*, London, Routledge and Kegan Paul, 1951, p. 26; "Crazy Jane to the Bishop".

37. Teilhard de Chardin, p. 288.

38. Charles O. McDonald (*"Decorum, Ethos*, and *Pathos* in the Heroes of Elizabethan Tragedy, with Particular Reference to *Hamlet*," *JEGP*, LXI, 1962, 330–48), in the process of refuting the persistent idea that a failure of psychological consistency should be considered a defect in tragic dramatic structure, makes the good and relevant point: ". . . it is the *breaking* of that *ethic* pattern by *pathos*, the passionate, irrational, illogical, apsychological, unexpected, that creates the real impact of tragedy." (p. 237) McDonald's book *The Rhetoric of Tragedy* (Univ. of Massachusetts Press, 1966) provides a wealth of evidence from rhetoric, both as a language phenomenon and as a systematically developed art form, for that "antilogistic" bias which both sophistry and tragedy found congenial.

39. "The Possibility of a Christian Tragedy," *Thought*, p. 406; in *Tragedy: Modern Essays in Criticism*, p. 212.

40. William James, letter to H. G. Wells, Sept. 11, 1906. Cited from *The Letters of William James* (ed. H. James), Boston, Atlantic Monthly Press, 1930, 2 vols., II, 260.

41. Erich Frank, *Philosophical Understanding and Religious Truth*, New York, Oxford Univ. Press, 1945, p. 11.

42. Norman Rabkin (*Shakespeare and the Common Understanding*, New York, Free Press, 1967), while conceding that "it would be wrong to extrapolate from the physicist's predicament to grandiose generalizations about the split nature of reality," provides a brilliantly sustained use of Bohr's and Oppenheimer's "principle of complementarity" to turn to positive account the dialectic, ambivalence, ambiguity he finds pervasive in Shakespeare. It is a strategy of *both/and:* workable, if not

meaningful, accommodations can be made of "phenomena on a large scale"—e.g., the "values" displayed in dramatic action in Shakespeare—without having to descend into the contradictory and subversive behavior of the particular atoms, the paradoxical-ironic words; "we live easily with complementary answers." Perhaps the practical scientists and the social engineers and the art-of-the-possible working politicians manage so; but the very persistence with which the philosopher-scientists return to and worry the problem makes one wonder whether using the tactics of *as if* really enables them to keep their "epistemological predicament" safely on the hither side of dilemma.

43. Teilhard de Chardin, pp. 277, 288; Richmond Y. Hathorn, *Tragedy, Myth, and Mystery*, Bloomington, Indiana Univ. Press, 1962, p. 185; E. L. B. Cherbonnier, "Biblical Faith and the Idea of Tragedy," *The Tragic Vision and the Christian Faith* (ed. Nathan A. Scott), New York, Association Press, 1957, p. 28; Wyndham Lewis, *The Writer and the Absolute*, London, Methuen, 1952, p. 39.

44. *A Definition of Tragedy*, New York, New York Univ. Press, 1961, p. 165. Although Mandel's "definition" of literary tragedy fails, I think, to be completely convincing and he too softens into saying that "success, indeed, is the feeling of success," he has collected, under the rubric of "tragic reality," a formidable array of hard-core and hard-nosed, recalcitrant and recurrent formulas. See especially pp. 162–68.

45. Robert Warshow, *The Immediate Experience*, New York, Doubleday, 1954, pp. 127–33.

46. Mandel, p. 166.

47. Cited from *Twentieth Century Writing* (ed. W. Stafford), New York, Odyssey, 1965, pp. 564, 551, 554.

Even the high-minded enterprise of assigning critical praise or blame to artists themselves (not to mention its more frivolous cousin, book-reviewing) seems to be condemned to the winners-and-losers competition: even Addison, says Pope (in delicately conditional clauses, as he builds the successful rhymed couplet, weeping crocodile tears), can bear no brother near the throne and must hate him for arts that caused himself to rise. Or, in what one is accustomed to think of as the spacious, room-for-all Elizabethan Age, we find that Ralegh, wishing to endow Spenser with "living fame"—that last infirmity of noble mind—is impelled to denigrate Petrarch and threaten Homer to do so ("Methought I saw the grave where Laura lay").

48. Laurence Lerner, "Tragedy: Religious and Humanist," *REL*, 2, 1961, 28–37; 31; Reinhold Niebuhr, *Beyond Tragedy*, New York,

Scribners, 1937, pp. 45, 18; *The Nature and Destiny of Man,* New York, Scribners, 1941, p. 16; Jones, *On Aristotle and Greek Tragedy* (New York, Oxford Univ. Press, 1962), p. 94.

The infinite regressiveness of effectual righteousness escapes from the apparent container of the Gospel parable of the Pharisee and the Publican to the ironic realm of parody: a Pastor and a Minister of Education on their knees crying out, "O Lord, I am nothing!" are joined by the Janitor of the church; whereupon the Minister nudges the Pastor and says, "Now look who thinks *he's* nothing!" It is instructive, however, of the way black-humor demons can be whitewashed that the latest version of this story has turned up in a feature called "Laughter is the Best Medicine" in *The Reader's Digest* (August 1968, p. 112).

49. I accept this attribution from Webster's *Second International Dictionary,* s.v. "poetic, poetical justice."

50. Mircea Eliade (*Mephistophilis and the Androgyne,* New York, Sheed & Ward, 1956) is helpful here in pointing out that the central function of paradox and metaphor is "to make the outside like the inside"—in our terms, the container like the thing contained—and that this leads logically to an identifying of God and Satan; *evil* becomes a relative term.

Metaphor, of course, is the most intriguing, the most fearsome, the most inclusive of language-concepts, and thereby most amenable to exploitation by the tragic. Consider the implications of the following remarks, chosen almost at random: the radical acceptance of metaphor involves one in "the ontological status of paradox—an acceptance, that is to say, of the view that paradox lies inextricably at the very heart of reality" (Philip Wheelwright, *Heraclitus,* quoted by Jackson I. Cope, *The Metaphoric Structure of "Paradise Lost",* Baltimore, Johns Hopkins Press, 1962, p. 5.) "Metaphor is really metamorphosis . . . this is my body" (Norman O. Brown, *Love's Body,* p. 168.) For Brown, the duality-principle supersedes, indeed is the true, reality-principle; "James Joyce and his daughter, crazy Lucia, these two are one. The God is Dionysus, the mad truth" (p. 160). M. G. Cooke ("From Comedy to Terror," *Massachusetts Review,* Spring 1968, 331–43) credits Joyce with the "singularly modern articulation of the possibilities of the short story form, giving it an ostensibly casual, free-moving, even a metamorphic structure, instead of the old teleological structure" (334), and finds that the stories show us "a complex that is, putting us under the obligation of maintaining a plural consciousness of disharmonious states caught in . . . a single metamorphic pattern" (340). (Cooke's whole article is incidentally illuminating for our study of Faulkner as a tragedian, ch. 4.) The attempt to convert metaphor (the principle of duality, interchangeability, mutability) into metamorphosis is at the heart of such would-be transcendences of the tragic as *The Faerie Queene.*

51. William Empson, *The Structure of Complex Words*, London, Chatto & Windus; New York, New Directions, 1951; Wolfgang Clemen, *The Development of Shakespeare's Imagery*, New York, Hill and Wang, 1962 [Harvard, 1951 (?)]. First published as *Shakespeares Bilder*, Bonn, 1936; Edward A. Armstrong, *Shakespeare's Imagination*, Lincoln, Univ. of Nebraska Press, 1963, first published in 1946 by Lindsay Drummond Limited; Caroline Spurgeon, *Shakespeare's Imagery and What It Tells Us*, Cambridge, Eng., Cambridge Univ. Press, 1935; M. M. Mahood, *Shakespeare's Wordplay*, London, Methuen, 1957, pp. 20, 168.

52. "It is remarkable that the Greeks seem to have had an instinctive horror of the very logic which it was obviously their mission to develop: for Aeschylus uses *synthetoi logoi* in the sense of mere 'fictions', which are, he says, 'of all things most hateful to the gods.' " Owen Barfield, *Poetic Diction* (New York, McGraw-Hill, 1952), p. 191, n. 1.

53. Sister Miriam Joseph, C.S.C., *Rhetoric in Shakespeare's Time*, New York, Harcourt, Brace, 1962, pp. 398, 333, 334.

54. Mahood p. 73.

55. Donald Davie, *Articulate Energy—An Enquiry into the Syntax of English Poetry*, New York, Harcourt, Brace, 1955.

Their cohorts, the transformational-generative grammarians, are using terms and formulas which at least do not contradict our notions: deep structure, surface structure, transforms (all of which are real mental events); the surface structure determines phonetic form, the deep structure determines meaning.

56. *Antony and Cleopatra*, II.v.50–53.

57. Francis Christensen, making a case for the primacy of the cumulative sentence and the importance of word-clusters, cites the novelist John Erskine: "What you say is found not in the noun but in what you add to qualify the noun. . . . The noun, the verb, and the main clause serve merely as the base on which meaning will rise. . . . The modifier is the essential part of any sentence." Christensen, "A Generative Rhetoric of the Sentence," in *Contemporary Essays on Style* (ed. Glenn A. Love and Michael Payne), Glenview, Ill., Scott, Foresman and Co., p. 29.

58. Davie, p. 25.

59. The language of the King James Version of the Old Testament deploys these vibrations in, for example, the story of Jacob's daring attempt to bring into actuality the Lord's metamorphosis of the "rights" of elder and younger:

[Blind Isaac asks, "Who art thou, my son?"]
And Jacob said unto his father, I am Esau thy firstborn . . .
And Isaac said unto Jacob, Come near, I pray thee, that I may *feel* thee, my son, whether thou be my *very* son Esau or not . . .
And he discerned him not, because his hands were hairy, *as* his brother Esau's hands: so he blessed him.
And he said, Art thou my *very* son Esau? And he said, I am . . . and he smelled the smell of his raiment, and blessed him, and said, *See*, the smell of my son *is as the smell* of a field which the Lord hath blessed: *therefore* . . . cursed be everyone that curseth thee, and blessed be every one that blesseth thee.
And it came to pass, *as soon as* Isaac had made an end of his blessing Jacob, and Jacob was *yet scarce* gone out from the presence of his father that Esau . . . came in . . .
And he said, I am thy son, thy firstborn, Esau.
And Jacob *trembled very exceedingly*, and said, Who?
And . . . Esau cried with a *great and exceeding bitter cry* . . .
And [Isaac] said, Thy brother came with *subtlety*, and hath taken away the blessing.
And he said, Is he not *rightly named* Jacob? for he hath supplanted me these two times . . .
And Esau hated Jacob *because of* the blessing wherewith his father blessed him: and Esau said in his heart . . . then will I slay my brother Jacob. (*Genesis* 27:18–41; emphasis added.)

60. Frank, p. 11; Niebuhr, *Beyond Tragedy*, pp. 40, 41; Mandel, pp. 164, 166, 168; Elder, p. 54.

61. Hathorn, pp. 178–79.

62. Lionel Abel, who has, I believe, penetrated to many essential differences between tragedy and "metatheatre," still clings to rationalism and "taste" (which the Greeks had "assuredly" but Shakespeare was deficient in) as the essentials of tragic drama (or dramatic tragedy; for him the terms seem to be interchangeable): "If, as Kant has it, there is radical evil in the universe, then a bad daemon ought to be possible. Rational thought has to deny this, and dramatic thinking has never been

able to present a daemonic devil on the stage. . . . The Greeks . . . excluded villains from the tragic universe." But who or what could be more villainous, and daemonic, than Dionysus, or the Furies, or Medea —or Phaedra (or Antigone!) in the clutches of merciless Aphrodite? If we can momentarily detach tragic thinking from rational thought, dramatic modes, and other such containers, it should not be too difficult to move from the ambivalence of the Coleridgean "daemonic sublime" through various demon/daemon, hermaphrodite-andogyne concepts to the state of affairs close to our formula, where the very act of transcendence becomes the ill-fated protagonist of the tragic action; witness, for example, Eliade (op. cit., p. 123):

> Every attempt to transcend the opposites carries with it a certain danger. This is why the ideas of a *coincidentia oppositorum* always arouse ambivalent feelings; on the one side, man is haunted by the desire to escape from his particular situation and regain a transpersonal mode of life; on the other, he is paralyzed by the fear of losing his "identity" and "forgetting" himself.

Or Jung (*Answer to Job*, p. 178):

> The unconscious wants to flow into consciousness in order to reach the light, but at the same time it continually thwarts itself, because it would rather remain unconscious. That is to say, God wants to become man, but not quite.

Angus Fletcher (*Allegory*, Ithaca, Cornell Univ. Press, 1964, *passim*, notably ch. I, "The Daemonic Agent") provides a wealth of argument and documentation on the notion of the divisive devilish demonic daemon.

63. *King Lear*, IV.ii.46–51.

64. Richard Hooker, universally acclaimed since Walton's *Life* as both a controversialist of mild and sweet reasonableness and a theologian who found the middle way between natural law and authoritarian scripture, betrays this uneasiness and irritability as soon as he gets down to particulars: he browbeats his opponents as "vulgar" and "brutish" for daring to challenge his position; and not all his casuistry and his "therefores" can insulate him from his own quasi-tragic vision of metaphysical evil:

> It hath already been showed how all things necessary unto salvation, in such sort as before we have maintained, must needs be possible for men to know, and that many things are in such sort necessary, the

knowledge whereof is by the light of nature impossible to be attained. Whereupon it followeth that either all flesh is excluded from possibility of salvation, which to think were most barbarous, or else that God hath by supernatural means revealed the way of life so far as doth suffice. (*Ec. Pol.*, Bk. I, ch. 14)

[A sufficiently desperate conclusion, this *or else*.]

The first principles of the law of nature are easy: hard it were to find men ignorant of them, but concerning the duty which Nature's law doth require at the hands of men in a number of things particular, so far have the natural understanding even of sundry whole nations been darkened, that they have not discerned—no, not gross iniquity—to be sin. Again, being so prone as we are to fawn upon ourselves, and to be ignorant as much as may be of our own deformities, without the feeling sense whereof we are most wretched, even so much the more because not knowing them we cannot as much as desire to have them taken away, how should our festered sores be cured, but that God hath delivered a law as sharp as the two-edged sword, piercing the very closest and most unsearchable corners of the heart which the law of nature can hardly, human laws by no means possible, reach unto? (*Ec. Pol.*, Bk. I, ch. 12)

[Not only the question-begging, but the irritable reaching after words to express a conviction of malaise, hardly persuade one of the writer's being at ease in the Anglican Zion.]

65. C. G. Jung, *Answer to Job* (trans. R. F. C. Hull), Cleveland and New York, World, 1960.

Albert S. Cook's perceptive monograph (*The Root of the Thing*, Bloomington, Indiana Univ. Press, 1968) on the verbal strategy of *Job*, in which *all* agonists in the debate—Job, the comforters, Elihu, and Jehovah—participate by anticipation in the final *détente*, reinforces this view.

66. See note 23 for ch. 1.

67. J. A. Bryant (*Hippolyta's View*, Lexington, Kentucky Univ. Press, 1961) uses Augustine's vision of the world as "a fair field, fresh with the odor of Christ's name," as the start of a kind of sorites: this world-view was common in Shakespeare's day; it was often used in sermons; sermons employed typology; typology influenced the thinking of practically all Elizabethans, literate or illiterate; typology was genuinely sacramental; consciously or unconsciously, "Shakespeare was

a genuine typologist in his use of Scriptural allusion and analogy." I am not sure what *genuine* means in the last member of this logical progression; but it is a good example of the inference-deduction-implication technique employed by many apologists for a Christian Shakespeare: the notions of order and hierarchy were promulgated officially in *The Book of Homilies* and in mandatory sermons; therefore, everybody believed and accepted them; therefore, Shakespeare must have been a genuine proponent of order and hierarchy. The massive evidence for a contrary effect compiled by such investigators as Hiram Haydn (*The Counter-Renaissance*) and D. C. Allen (*Doubt's Boundless Sea*) has still to be come to terms with. And what of the elementary observation that, if the world was indeed a fair sacrament and the social and political hierarchy not only God-ordained but delightful for everybody, why did the polity of both church and state resort to such drastic means of persuasion as to require the sermons to be preached throughout the Christian year and require everyone to go and listen to them?

Raymond Southall (*The Courtly Maker*, New York, Barnes & Noble, 1964, pp. 55–56) demonstrates that a prior generation (the early Tudor court poets) are not susceptible of Bryant's kind of inference: "There is then in the poetry of the courtly makers another equally traditional attitude towards the world, one which sees existence as an extremely precarious business, an attitude far more consistent with the realities of life at Court than that propounded in *The Book of Homilies*."

68. P. 133.

69. Eliade (p. 91) provides an analogue from a different tradition: "One of the most frequent prayers [in Vedic texts] is to be 'delivered from Varuna'.... And yet the worshipper cries, 'When shall I at last be with Varuna?'" Niebuhr cites the Psalmist, "Enter *not* into judgment with thy servant, for in thy sight is no man living justified!" Hopkins expands on "Thou are indeed just, Lord, if I contend With thee; but, sir, so what I plead is just," but ends his sonnet on a note of deprivation and a plea for mercy, not justice. Donne finds to his bewilderment and terror that he is more damnable than the world of nature, which (in his selection, at least) has no odor of sanctity about it but is composed of poisonous minerals, death-dealing trees, lecherous goats, and envious serpents. He must be battered, broken, divorced, imprisoned, and ravished if he is ever to be a free denizen of God's kingdom come on earth.

It has been frequently noted that the Decalogue is mainly a series of prohibitions, not commandments, given, as Paul says in *Galatians* 3, as a supplement to the promises to Abraham "in view of transgressions of it." The Law was promulgated to curb the desires of the flesh, which are deadly to the spirit: the Law is the ministry of death, the ministry of condemnation. If the Spirit of the New Covenant, the positive commandment "Thou shalt love," is indeed the ministry of justification, why does the Lord's Prayer end with a plea to be spared that trial which must invoke the letter that kills?

70. One might expect to find instead Euripides's *Bacchae*, as the ultimate (in time and in exigency) Greek treatment of theodicy-centered tragedy. I have chosen not to use it, partly because of its having gone almost "beyond tragedy" (even Euripidean) so as to be un-representative, and because the ground has been traversed so often already. Thomas G. Rosenmayer's "*Bacchae* and *Ion*: Tragedy and Religion" (which, though it was a chapter of his *The Masks of Tragedy*, Austin, Univ. of Texas Press, 1963, I did not encounter until its reprinting in *Moderns on Tragedy*, ed. Lionel Abel, Greenwich, Fawcett, 1967, 152–74) has anticipated my central trope in this connection, e.g.: "the violently intrusive character of the Dionysiac life, of the unlimited thrusting itself into the limited and exploding its stale equilibrium" (Abel, 157–58); "a class of images . . . : the container filled to the bursting point . . . as the play advances, containment proves inadequate" (165); "Dionysus disrupts the settled life, he cracks the shell of civic contentment and isolation" (166); "In the *Bacchae*, *hybris* is quite literally the 'going beyond,' the explosion of the unlimited across the barriers which a blind civilization has erected in the vain hope of keeping shut out what it does not wish to understand" (166). I would add to Rosenmayer's powerful reading only some recognition that even here, in the triumphant apotheosis of the Thing Contained, it displays some of the corruption (cruelty, petulance) of the Container it shatters in the process.

71. When Arrowsmith addressed himself directly to Euripides and his tragic ambience he presented what I think is an ironclad case for the final Greek experience of "hard" tragedy—inclusive of Thucydides and the Glory That Was Greece ("A Greek Theater of Ideas," 1964); reprinted in *Euripides: A Collection of Critical Essays* (ed. Erich Segal), Englewood Cliffs, N. J., Prentice-Hall, Inc., 1968, pp. 13-33).

72. William Arrowsmith, "The Criticism of Greek Tragedy," *Tulane Drama Review*, III, 3, March 1959. Repr. in *Tragedy: Vision and Form* (ed. R. W. Corrigan), San Francisco, Chandler, 1965, 317-42; q.v., pp. 328, 330, 332, 335, 334, 332.

73. Mandel, ch. 6, pp. 31 ff.

74. Freud, *Beyond the Pleasure Principle*. Cited from A. C. Outler, "Freud and the Domestication of Tragedy," in Scott, p. 271.

75. See note 20 for ch. 1.

76. Hathorn, p. 109; Arrowsmith, p. 331.

77. John Jones transfers all the blame for this to the interpreters: critics' attempts to rationalize it cheapen the issue "by a procedure which is as slovenly as it is dishonest" (p. 107). He points out that Athena's action as goddess-judge (the bad rationalization, the programmatic dream of innocence) is countermanded by what he calls the "dramatic" *fact* that Orestes is still polluted, still dripping blood (p. 106). But Jones goes on: "Aeschylus accepts and respects this simple continuity, . . . lives within it and imagines through it. . . . He returns the answers yea and no to our question 'Is he guilty?' This means a resolute containment of revenge" (p. 107). Jones's collocation of *containment* and *resoluteness* is fortuitous for my argument. He too sees what is going on, and indeed almost makes the point in my terms—that the "Aeschylean norm" is a container, that Aristotle's "ideal was one of tight, box-like containment" (p. 162). He sees the "something thin and 'mental' in Agamemnon's argument [in Euripides's *Iphigenia at Aulis*] and his gummed-on patriotic sentiment" (p. 261)—but won't attribute the same thing (from much the same kind of evidence) to Aeschylus's Athena and Apollo. At the end he relapses into a lyrical, and only pseudo-critical, piety: "A transformation of curse into blessing crowns the *Oresteia*, natural and prodigious, like a snowfall in the night to the morrow's wakers" (p. 136).

78. Arrowsmith, pp. 333, 334.

79. C. J. Sisson, *Shakespeare's Tragic Justice*, London, Methuen, 1964, p. 59.

80. Cited from H. D. F. Kitto, *Form and Meaning in Drama*, London, Methuen, 1956, pp. 41–42.

81. John Jones, *On Aristotle and Greek Tragedy*, New York, Oxford Univ. Press, 1962, p. 103.

82. (*Choephoroe*) Jones's version, p. 131.

83. Kafka, *The Great Wall of China*. Cited from J. Hillis Miller, "Franz Kafka and the Metaphysics of Alienation," in Scott, pp. 282, 293, 298.

84. See Eduard Geismar's *Lectures on the Religious Thought of Søren Kierkegaard* (Minneapolis, Augsburg Publishing House, 1938) for a trenchant critique of "reasonable theology." Much of what he says about Christians—e.g., "When theologians develop a system of

apologetics for the purpose of defending Christianity, they make a fatal mistake. . . . Such defense, even though well meant, is an unconscious betrayal"—can apply also to non-Christian tragic theodicizers. The (perverse) obverse of this coin can be found in D. H. Lawrence, who faults Aeschylus in that, although he has provided "the intoxicating satisfaction of the Oresteian trilogy," "he still adheres to the law. . . . What he has learned of Love, he does not yet quite believe" (*P* 476, *P* 482). These references, to Lawrence's *Phoenix*, have been gleaned from David J. Gordon's most helpful monograph, *D. H. Lawrence as a Literary Critic*, New Haven, Yale Univ. Press, 1966, p. 87. Gordon remarks, apropos of this high-water mark of Lawrence's "Quarrel with Tragedy," that "What Lawrence is after in this essay [on Hardy], and the standard by which he finds all tragedy wanting, cannot itself reasonably be called tragedy at all." I agree, but not for Gordon's reasons. Lawrence, like most radical Romanticists, is waylaid by innocence, strength, vitalism, pity. Gordon, while faithfully and perceptively demonstrating Lawrence's biases, seems to restrict himself to various "modal" containers for the idea of tragedy that he finds Lawrence falling short of. Recognizing all this, however, should not blind us to the important service Lawrence rendered tragic theory in identifying the "intrinsic" demon, and in insisting that "closed form" was "a cul-de-sac" (p. 49). "If it be really a work of art, it must contain the essential criticism on the morality to which it adheres" (*P* 476; Gordon, p. 45): a typical Lawrencean "transvaluation" of the conventional ideas of morality and immorality, of container and thing contained.

85. C. J. Sisson (*Shakespeare's Tragic Justice*, London, Methuen, 1964), recognizing that a "complex and thorny exegesis" of these and other such passages has to assume "that Heaven's direction of events would contemplate the shedding of innocent blood as part of its plan," rejects it because it "raises more difficulties than it solves" (pp. 105–106). This inability to contemplate the possibility that Shakespeare *was* questioning Providence is a consequence, perhaps, of Sisson's adherence to Professor Herford's "practical sagacity" as against "imaginative intuition" (p. 54) in reading Shakespeare. He craves (as we all doubtless do) more "comfort" (p. 8) than can be found in *hamartia* and cannot remain in a state of uncertainty: "Yet some satisfaction of our sense of justice is necessary if the tragic emotions are not to be heightened and to remain unresolved in a final disharmony" (p. 10). [This is a stubborn vestige of the kind of a priori and non sequitur watering down of the tragic idea that had its classic statement in John Dennis's 1712

Essay on the Genius and Writings of Shakespeare: "But indeed Shakespeare has been wanting in the exact distribution of poetical justice . . . in most of his best tragedies. . . . The good and the bad then perishing promiscuously in the best of Shakespeare's tragedies, there can be either none or very weak instructions in them: *for* such promiscuous events call the government of providence into question, and by skeptics and libertines are resolved into chance." (emphasis added)] But practical sagacity, "resting upon knowledge and observation," does not effectually guard Professor Sisson from finding the "true significance of Hamlet's action and words in the Prayer scene" to be Hamlet's recognition that the King is in sanctuary: "To kill him now would be sacrilege." Thus is Hamlet saved to be the worthy minister of a comfortingly just Heaven.

86. "Is There a Tragic Sense of Life?" *Commentary*, December 1964, p. 35.

87. That this sentiment, if indeed it is to be taken seriously, is a product of a theologizing, Job's-counselor, official capturing of the gods to justify one's own purposes than a genuine recognition of their sovereignty, is suggested by Shakespeare's putting it, in relatively dry, rhetorically righteous terms, into the mouths of special pleaders:

POMPEY: If the great gods be just, they shall assist
               The deeds of justest men.
MENECRATES: Know, worthy Pompey,
               That what they do delay, they not deny.
               . . . .   We, ignorant of ourselves,
               Beg often our own harms, which the wise powers
               Deny us for our good. So find we profit
               By losing of our prayers.
POMPEY: Be't as our gods will have't! It only stands
               Our lives upon to use our strongest hands.

And Antony too betrays the insincerity of his *argumentum ad foeminam* by spouting it again, in accents that are not his:

ANTONY: You have been a boggler ever.
               But when we in our viciousness grow hard—
               Oh, misery on't—the wise gods seel our eyes,
               And in our own filth drop our clear judgments, make us
               Adore our errors, laugh at's while we strut
               To our confusion.

And what are we to make of the sly implications of using the same tune in *Macbeth:*

BANQUO: But 'tis strange.
And oftentimes, to win us to our harm,
The instruments of darkness tell us truths,
Win us with honest trifles, to betray's
In deepest consequence

at the very moment when fair and foul are inextricably mixed, when "supernatural soliciting Cannot be ill, cannot be good . . . and nothing is But what is not"? It is a hair-raising surmise.

88. *Metatheatre*, New York, Hill and Wang, 1963, pp. 23–24, 12.

89. See M. M. Mahood, *Poetry and Humanism* (London, Cape, 1950, p. 69), for the "corrollaries" of Faustus's texts and a discussion of the consequences of their suppression.

90. Yeats, "Shepherd and Goatherd," cited from Reid, p. 116; Aldous Huxley, "Tragedy and the Whole Truth," in *Collected Essays*, New York, Harper and Row, 1959, p. 99; Elizabeth Sewell, *The Orphic Voice*, New Haven, Yale Univ. Press, 1960, p. 350.

91. Simone Weil, "Beyond Personalism," (trans. Russell S. Young), *Cross Currents*, II, 3, Spring 1952, 59–76; 71. Written in London in 1942; originally appeared in *La Table Ronde*, 1950.

92. See Guthke's marshalling of testimony from writer-theorists (Pirandello, Ionesco, Dürrenmatt, et al.) on the act of writing as an exercise in courage, as therapy. He admits their pessimism and nihilism, but bases it on "a deeply troubled skepticism, perhaps, but one which still asks questions and thus lives up to its genuine function" (*Modern Tragicomedy*, p. 170). D. H. Lawrence, while decrying conceptualization and even symbolic categories, still insisted that "the whole goal of the unconscious is incarnation and self-manifestation" (*Psychology and the Unconscious*, p. 16; cited from Gordon, p. 51).

2. SOME NEW READINGS IN SHAKESPEARE

1. Yeats, "Lapis Lazuli," cited from Reid, p. 154.

2. R. M. Adams, *Strains of Discord*, Ithaca, Cornell Univ. Press, 1958; Sewell, op. cit.; J. O. Perry, "The Relationship of Disparate Voices in Poems," *EIC*, XV, 1, January 1965, 49–64.

3. Hiram Haydn, *The Counter-Renaissance*, New York: Scribners,

1950; Robert Ornstein, *The Moral Vision of Jacobean Tragedy*, Madison, Univ. of Wisconsin Press, 1960; D. C. Allen, *Doubt's Boundless Sea*, Baltimore, Johns Hopkins Press, 1964; E. W. Talbert, *The Problem of Order*, Chapel Hill, Univ. of North Carolina Press, 1962.

4. Jonas Barish, "Shakespeare's Prose Style," in *Ben Jonson and the Language of Prose Comedy*, Cambridge, Mass., Harvard Univ. Press, 1960, repr. in *Approaches to Shakespeare* (ed. Norman Rabkin), New York, McGraw-Hill, 1964, pp. 245–63; Krieger, op. cit; Wilfrid Watson, "Tarquin, the Master-Mistress, and the Dark Lady," *Humanities Association Bulletin*, XV, 2, Autumn 1964, 7–16; Jan Kott, *Shakespeare Our Contemporary* (trans. Boselaw Taborski), Garden City, N. Y., Doubleday, 1964; A. P. Rossiter, *Angel With Horns*, New York, Theatre Arts; London, Longmans, Green, 1961.

5. That is, what I take to be his deepest intuitions. Like all of us, he too feels compelled to find frameworks—"dialectic," for the Histories, or the old idea that in tragedy "greatness is asserted in destruction" (p. 42), or the implication that since the histories are "obscure tragedy," tragedy itself is somehow redeemed from obscurity. When he moves into his demonstration (pun intended), however, the radicalness comes through powerfully. *English Drama from Early Times to the Elizabethans*, Rossiter's 1950 study which finds evidence of ambivalence, equivocation, "the undermining negative," "rituals of negation," etc. as central in the *pre*-Elizabethan dramatic tradition, has recently been reissued (New York, Barnes & Noble, 1967 BN 49).

6. Letter to George and Thomas Keats (21 December 1817); to Woodhouse, 27 October 1818.

7. The Elizabethans probably pronounced it more like *no-thing*. Samuel Daniel rhymes it with *loathing*, and Shakespeare, in Sonnet 20, with *a-doting;* there are several puns with *noting* in *Much Ado About Nothing*.

8. The essential absurdity of the casuistical words and actions of the "mad kings" in *King John* is given voice by that fair affliction, Constance, who moves with virtuosity through the seven modes of quarreling but is most devastating with the Lie Direct:

K. Phi. The yearly course that brings this day about
         Shall never see it but a holiday.
Con.   A wicked day, and not a holy day!
         . . . .

Nay, rather turn this day out of the week,
This day of shame, oppression, perjury.
. . . .

You have beguiled me with a counterfeit
  Resembling majesty . . .
Let not the hours of this ungodly day
Wear out the day in peace, but, ere sunset,
  Set armed Discord 'twixt these perjured Kings!
Hear me, oh, hear me!

Aust.   Lady Constance, peace!
Con.   War! War! No peace! Peace is to me a war. (III.i.81–112)

9. *Angel With Horns*, pp. 260–61. The most thoroughgoing and convincing analysis of this part of the process that I know of is Norman
Rabkin's application of the "complementarity principle" (see note 42,
above). He demonstrates (without having to restrict himself to the
"tragedies") a constant mode of duality, which displays itself variously
as ambivalent, problematic, dialectic—and, most commonly, as dramatic. What keeps me from endorsing this most illuminating critical
stance completely, on the present occasion, is that it does restrict itself
to (even) these *containers* and does not dwell for long on the thing(s)
contained. For example, the theme of *Troilus and Cressida* is said to
concern a time indifferent to our purposes and values (p. 54); the
competing elements of the debates between Hector and Troilus,
Achilles and Ulysses, Greeks and Trojans, are assumed as equally
valid. But I would find that the debate or dialectic is frame, and that
in the process *of* debate (as well as through the erosion of time) the
values themselves are corroded and shown to carry the seeds of their
own destruction.

Rossiter too commits himself to working within the equational, bi-
polar container ("Ambivalence: The Dialectic of the Histories"); it is
only when he (and Rabkin) gets down to particulars that the plunge
toward the sardonic and the absurd is seen. As long as equal time is
given to both sides of a dialectic and the amenities are preserved, containment results. "We live easily with complementary answers." But
the uneasy demon of risibility is still there: Caliban has been taught
language, and his profit on't is he knows how to curse.

10. A. C. Bradley, *Shakespearean Tragedy*, 2nd. ed., London, Macmillan, 1932, p. 439.

11. Mahood, *Shakespeare's Wordplay*, pp. 25–29, 47.

12. Kitto, p. 254.

13. Mahood, p. 164.

14. G. Wilson Knight, *The Crown of Life*, London, Methuen, 1947, p. 112.

15. I use the New Arden text, edited by Kenneth Muir. It is recommended that the scenes be read through now, as presented, before continuing with my commentary.

16. Sisson, pp. 16, 26.

17. There is a preview of this trope and of its usefulness as a vehicle for the tragic idea of fatal entanglement, in *Romeo and Juliet;* two households, both alike in dignity, contribute equally to new mutiny, "Where civil blood makes civil hands unclean." Benvolio's "discovery" to the Prince of the unlucky manage of the fatal brawl between Tybalt and Mercutio emphasizes that even newly-converted Romeo's respective lenity

> Could not take truce with the unruly spleen
> Of Tybalt deaf to peace, but that he tilts
> With piercing steel at bold Mercutio's breast,
> Who, all as hot, turns *deadly point to point*,
> And, with a martial scorn, with one hand beats
> Cold death aside and with other sends
> It back to Tybalt, whose dexterity
> Retorts it. . . .
> [Romeo's] agile arm beats down *their fatal points*
> And 'twixt them rushes. Underneath whose arm
> An envious thrust from Tybalt hit the life
> Of stout Mercutio . . .

Prince Escalus asks, "Who now the price of his dear blood doth owe?" At the outset of the play he had called them *all* "Rebellious subjects, . . . Profaners of this neighbor-stained steel"; at the close, "Where be these enemies?"

Some ramifications suggest themselves. (1) In (the early) *Romeo and Juliet* Shakespeare is probing the idea of *confusion* as a still-obscure instrument of tragedy (Friar Laurence can say, though unavailingly, "Confusion's cure lives not in these confusions"); Prince Escalus, though he has a bosom "interest" in their hate's proceeding, still can tell fair from foul, temper from distemper, and acknowledge the rightness of his own punishment. In *Macbeth*, ambition-engendered confusion makes his masterpiece, with King Duncan rejoicing in the indistinguishability of death-dealing comparisons so long as *his* bosom interest is served. This is penetration and development, in depth, into confines of tragedy unplumbed before.

(2) Schemes and tropes feed (and feed on) one another in Shakespeare. Kittredge restored the Folio punctuation of the *Macbeth* line ("Point against point, rebellious arm 'gainst arm") from Theobald's unaccountable shift of the comma to after *rebellious*, but, apparently to Dover Wilson's approval, added that "'rebellious arm' refers (of course) to Sweno's." Yet, Wilson also records Simpson's discovery that the Folio reading is in line with "a characteristic feature of Shakespeare's style," substantiated by the following citations:

KJ, 2.1.390. [Bastard]   That done, dissever your united strengths,
                         And part your mingled colours once again,
                         Turn face to face and *bloody point to point.*
                         . . .
                         How like you this wild counsel, mighty
                            States?
                         Smacks it not something of the policy?

R.II, 1.1.16   Face to face,
                         And *frowning brow to brow*, ourselves will
                            hear
                         The accused and the accuser freely speak.

H.V, 5.2.30   Since then my office hath so far prevailed
                         That, face to face and *royal eye to eye*
                         You here congreeted . . .

Add one more variation, from *Hamlet*, 5.2.60–62,

                         'Tis dangerous when the baser nature comes
                         Between the pass and *fell incensed points*
                         Of mighty opposites . . .

and a magnetic field of tragic statement is opened up and partially delineated. Point is counterpoint; and though they be both right royal, they are mutually bloody, deadly, fatal, and incriminatory.

18. For a succinct demonstration of how the words *are* the action in the *Oresteia* ("What is said next is what happens next"), see E. T. Owen, *The Harmony of Aeschylus* (Toronto, Clark, Irwin, 1952), ch. V. J. M. Nosworthy ("The Bleeding Captain Scene in *Macbeth*," *RES*, XXII, 1946, 126–30), while making a persuasive case for the scene

as authentically Shakespearean on the grounds of its being in the Sen-
ecan tradition of circumstantial, heroic narrative and its having many
echoes and parallels with the player's "Aeneas' tale to Dido" recitation
in *Hamlet*, still is content to say that it serves "no wider purpose than
that of presenting the events that precede Macbeth's first encounter
with the witches, and consequent assumption of the role of tragic hero.
Its scope is that of a prologue . . ." and that it "is one of the scenes most
likely to be curtailed, simply because it is not essential to the fabric of
the whole play." So far as I am aware, Nosworthy's reference (p. 127)
to "Kyd when he makes Andrea's ghost narrate the events that determine the action of *The Spanish Tragedy*," and two echoes in our
Macbeth scene of passages in *S. T.* I.i noted by G. Sarrazin in *Englische
Studien*, XXI, 1895 and picked up in the Furniss *Variorum*, are the only
recognitions of Kyd's play as exemplary here. Nosworthy is off in his
attribution: Andrea's "narration" takes place in the opening Chorus,
and is not like the *Macbeth* account of "how the battle went." Rather,
Andrea's ghost's setting the ensuing action in an infernal perspective is
closely parallel to the opening ("choral") scene of *Macbeth's* infernal
participants; and the subsequent reporting scenes in the two plays are
markedly similar in outward form and content. But Shakespeare so
concentrates and intensifies the inner ironies (of "blissful chivalry"
and worthy soldiership) as to make the scenes essential to the fabric of
the whole play, and to display the deeply tragic intrinsic knots of its
warp and woof.

19. The "turn of sympathy" at the center of Horace's "Cleopatra
Ode" (I.37) is accomplished by this same ambiguous figure:

mentemque lymphatam Mareotico
   redegit in veros timores
      Caesar ab Italia volantem

remis adurgens, *accipiter velut
mollis columbas aut leporem citus*
venator in campis nivalis
      Haemoniae, daret ut catenis

fatale monstrum; *quae generosius
perire* . . .

For a persuasive demonstration of how the *poetics* of the Ode accomplish the opposite of what it ostensibly started out to do (by a kind of

"overkill"—"the drunkenness that was a danger to be shunned, not emulated . . . is, as it were, overcompensated by the description of Caesar's eagerness to capture his now timorous victim. . . . our fear of her ferocity has been overcome by our realization of Caesar's"), see Brooks Otis, "A Reading of the Cleopatra Ode," *Arethusa*, I, 1 (Fall 1968), 47–61.

20. *Blood* has long been recognized as one of the central complex-word thematic vehicles of *Macbeth;* it is the sinister coupling of one of its group-variants (*wounds*) with *words* that is of particular interest here. Jones remarks of Orestes: "Seeing the Furies is proof of a kind of guilt, and having bloody hands evidences defilement . . . a culpable state of being continuous with its manifestations; there is a single term for both: pollution." Observing the appropriate distinction between Greek "metaphoric" compactness and Elizabethan-English "similistic" comparativeness, we find the same thing going on here: whether Duncan knows it or not (even whether Shakespeare knows it or not), to say that the captain's words *become* him as well as do his wounds—and in the same way—is to come dangerously near to polluting the report and its reporter. Bloody instructions, being taught, return to plague the inventor.

21. Sisson, *loc. cit.*

22. The theme of *Macbeth* is *the* imperial theme, and the two truths of the witches are "happy prologues" to its swelling act. They are devils' truths; yet Duncan is just as happy with them as is Macbeth. In Act IV scene iii, Malcolm and Macduff again try to determine what are, or should be, the king-becoming graces which make one fit to govern. But the list of virtues itself is subtly undermined by Macduff's coming back to the point of legitimacy as crucial—"O nation miserable! With an *untitled* tyrant bloody-sceptered"—and Malcolm's recognition that "a good and virtuous nature may recoil In an *imperial* charge." The debate, which tries to clear up both Malcolm's and Macduff's motivations, begins with suspicion:

Malcolm.   You have loved him [Macbeth] well . . .
Macduff.   I am not treacherous.
Malcolm.   But Macbeth is.

What indeed constitutes treason or treachery has been ominously canvassed several times earlier: by Banquo, who invokes it against Macbeth as he dies, and by Macduff's son, who brings it out in the open ("What is a traitor?") and points out the fatal consequences of the logical and semantic absurdity involved in the definition. Menteith, Caithness, Angus, Lenox, well-meaning lords and soldiers trying to find out how to "give obedience where 'tis truly owed," how at once to "dew the sovereign flower and drown the weeds," cannot really tell which is which: some say Macbeth (now "the tyrant") is mad; "others, that lesser hate him, Do call it valiant fury." The ambivalences of the opening scene persist. Malcolm's and Macduff's attempt to resolve them does no better:

> Malcolm. That which you are my thoughts cannot transpose:
> Angels are bright still, though the brightest fell:
> Though all things foul would wear the brows of grace,
> Yet Grace must still look so.

The colloquy ends with a reversion to the uncertainty of the opening:

> Macduff. Such welcome and unwelcome things at once
> 'Tis hard to reconcile.

Fair is still foul, foul fair.

Eric Bentley (*The Playwright as Thinker*, Cleveland, World Publishing Co., 1955—Meridian Book; first published 1946) gives us, in his assessment of Hebbel, a fine latter-day statement of this perennial tragic theme:

> Hebbel made of the dialectic of history a tragic, not merely a logical or meliorist, development. This is an admirable misunderstanding of Hegel and the cornerstone of Hebbelism. Into the abstract Hegelian mold he poured—with whatever philosophical impropriety—a poetry of his own. (p. 29)

An admirable misunderstanding of Hegel, by a nineteenth-century German, is a *felix culpa* indeed; it is too bad that "in a more explanatory mood he would explain that while there was no reconciliation, no poetic justice, there was a 'reconciliation of the Idea,' a vindication of the larger law to which the individual is subordinate." An admirable evasion of slavemaster man, to lay his vindictive disposition to the cause of an Idea. Aeschylus did no better.

23. *This* imperial theme was recognized, as early as *I. Henry VI*, as ineluctably tragic:

> Exeter. And now I fear that fatal prophecy
> Which in the time of Henry named the Fifth
> Was in the mouth of every sucking babe,

That Henry born at Monmouth should win all,
And Henry born at Windsor should lose all;
Which is so plain, that Exeter doth wish
His days may finish ere that hapless
time. (III.i.195–201)

The absoluteness of it, when the contention is for kingship (that absolute power whose mirror-image is corruption), is recognized by Richard II:

Ay, no; no, ay; for I must nothing be;
. . . .

Make me, that nothing have, with nothing grieved,
And thou with all pleased, that hast all achieved!
Long mayst thou live in Richard's seat to sit,
And soon lie Richard in an earthy pit!
(*Richard II*, IV.i.201–19)

D. A. Traversi comments, "*Nothing, nothing:* in the long run any relevant political conception will have to face the challenge implied in that word" (*Shakespeare: From Richard II to Henry V*, Stanford Univ. Press, 1957, p. 41).

24. L. C. Knights, "How Many Children Had Lady Macbeth?" (1933); repr. in *Explorations*, London, Chatto & Windus, 1936. The seminal intuitions of L. C. Knights—*Macbeth* as a dramatic poem, as a statement of evil; the power of details in providing a commentary upon the main interests aroused—will be recognized in much of the foregoing. The justification for saying them again is that Knights inexplicably fails to come up to, backs away from, or goes directly opposite to the intuitions in the rest of his essay. Likewise, another widely accepted and initially persuasive proposal of a central theme for *Macbeth*—Francis Fergusson's citation of "to outrun the pauser reason" in "*Macbeth* as the Imitation of an Action"—also fails or declines to admit the continual contamination by the images of "desperate and paradoxical struggle" of either the original "values" *or* the "good supernatural" at the end. ("*Macbeth* as the Imitation of an Action," *English Institute Essays*, New York, Columbia Univ. Press, 1952)

I should make the same kind of acknowledgment (and judgment) of John Holloway's treatment of this early scene and its connection with the rest of the play (*The Story of the Night*, Lincoln, Univ. of Nebraska Press, 1961, pp. 58 ff.). D. A. Traversi, reading *Macbeth* as "in the first place and above all, a play about the murder of a king" (*An Approach to Shakespeare*, Garden City, N. Y., Doubleday, 1956, p. 151), does not advert to the early scenes, and arrives at interpretations of the play almost opposite to mine; but in *Shakespeare: From Richard II to Henrvy V* he briefly develops some of the consequences of the use of charged language: "Two distinct intentions are, so to speak, superimposed upon one another and imperfectly unified. The first is purely formal, the development of an extended comparison to its logical conclusion; the second, springing apparently by chance from an idea contained in the simile, deviates the unfolding from its foreseen course." But Traversi seems to feel that this phenomenon needs explanation and apology: he calls it "a rhetorical elaboration, a conscious literary artifice, which is barely compatible with true dramatic effect"; *some* of the similes, which are "more closely related to true dramatic ends," show the emergence of "a poetic instrument adequate to the growing complexity of his intentions." (Pp. 109–11. This is apropos of *Henry IV, Part II*.)

25. Irving Ribner, rev., *Macbeth*, Waltham, Mass. Blaisdell, 1966, pp. vi, xvi.

26. Curtis B. Watson's *Shakespeare and the Renaissance Concept of Honor* (Princeton Univ. Press, 1960) is an extensive bid to recapture this whole area from those modern critics and interpreters who have (he thinks, ignorantly and unwarrantedly) dispensed themselves from the old view "that Shakespeare was a man of his age and that his plays reflect, with an inconsistency which has to be admitted and accepted, both the Christian and the pagan-humanist values of his period" (p. 6). He earnestly hopes to have provided "sure evidence that for the men of the Renaissance, including Shakespeare, a resonant sense of honor is in every respect excellent and never questionable" (p. 11). When he gets to demonstrating "Shakespeare's Ambivalent Use of Values" (chs. 8–9), one finds that "ambivalence and inconsistency" mean merely eclecticism in the gray areas where a "discrepancy between Christian and pagan-humanist attitudes" can be discerned (p. 327). Almost needless to say, I find such a concept of Shakespeare's "use" of values, and especially of "honor," willfully retrograde, and subversive of the proper study of both Shakespeare and tragedy.

27. D. J. Enright, for example, finds such designation debatable, in more ways than one ("*Coriolanus:* Tragedy or Debate?" *EIC*, IV, 1, 1954, 1–19). Michael McCanles ("The Dialectic of Transcendence in Shakespeare's *Coriolanus*," *PMLA*, LXXII, 1, March 1967, 44–53) dis-

plays many of the terms I have used, in Chapter I, as indices to the presence of the inner form of tragedy: inherent ambiguity, identity of apparent opposites, impossible situations, inexorable logic, *the very, both/and, exactly the same.* He uses them to set up what seem to me to be veritable paradigms for the play as tragedy:

> In other words, the condition of health in the state comes perilously close to causing its death. . . . What we watch is the inexorable working out of a love perverted into a drive toward power, from which few in the play seem redeemable [*because* Coriolanus's] transcendence corresponds to his destruction. . . . In short, Coriolanus can neither do without those he hates, nor can he do with those he "loves," and the play's final irony (it can hardly be called tragedy) is that these two are the same.

I should like to persuade Mr. McCanles that he has produced an almost flawless model of how it can hardly be called anything else.

28. Sisson, p. 16.

29. Henry V, in authorizing the execution of Bardolph for stealing a pax (with possible undertones of scapegoat-sacrifice, since Henry himself is in the process of "stealing the French peace"?), falls into a similar slip:

> We would have all such offenders so cut off. And we give express charge that in our marches through the country there be nothing compelled from the villages, nothing taken but paid for, none of the French upbraided or abused in disdainful language. *For* when lenity and cruelty play for a kingdom, the gentlest gamester is the soonest *winner.*

30. I am aware that much more than this can be done with Brutus (and the play) from the point of view of the psychoanalytical critics: e.g., *accounting for* his stuffiness, his obtuseness, etc., in terms of his being one of a composite son-brotherhood (Brutus, Cassius, Antony) rebelling against the father-figure Caesar, and so forth. I would suggest that it makes no difference: *tout comprendre* (even if *tout*, which is questionable) *n'est pas tout pardonner.*

31. Dean Frye, "The Question of Shakespearean 'Parody,'" *EIC,* XV, 1, January 1965, 22.

32. *The Peloponnesian Wars* may also be seen to be a ferocious exposure by the tragic imp of the naked aggression behind the democratic imperialism of Athens—the Athens of Pericles and Alcibiades, cradle of

Western civilization and culture; and one cannot forget, in reading the prologues to the departure of Henry V's navy from Southampton, that other scene of vainglorious setting-forth, the sendoff at Piraeus of the Athenian fleet for Syracuse.

33. Notably by D. A. Traversi (*Shakespeare from Richard II to Henry V*, California, Stanford Univ. Press, 1957); L. C. Knights (*Shakespeare: The Histories*, London, Longmans, Green, 1962); and H. M. Richmond (*Shakespeare's Political Plays*, New York, Random House, 1967).

34. Norman O. Brown, in *Love's Body* (p. 112), puts it thus: "The consequence of having a king is having a history, that is to say, wars; the purpose of which is to put down the historical action, the kings, of other peoples." Mircea Eliade (*Myths, Dreams and Mysteries*, New York, Harper, 1960, p. 200) concludes, from his study of military initiations in protohistorical Europe: "The warrior hero is not only a killer of dragons and other monsters, he is also a killer of men. The heroic duel is a sacrifice: war is a decadent ritual in which a holocaust of innumerable victims is offered up to the gods of victory."

35. A good example of what to me is blindness to the daemonic component in "form" is Rose A. Zimbardo's "The Formalism of *Henry V*," in *Shakespeare Encomium* (ed. Anne Paolucci), The City College Papers I (1964), 16–24. According to this reading, *Henry V* is "less a drama than a celebration . . . an almost perfect realization of meaning in form." As a paradigm of this, Miss Zimbardo quotes I.ii.241–243: "We are no tyrant [i.e., self-willed] but a Christian king [i.e., God-willed] / Unto whose grace our passion is as subject / As is our wretches fetter'd in our prisons." (Grace? *Our* wretches? *Our* prisons?) She finds that stylistic devices control action or passion which "might . . . disturb the measured order." Henry's challenge at Harfleur renders "the horrible subject matter . . . still as statuary" in stylistic formality through "balance, the use of triplets, and paramoron . . . enhanced by elevation and conventionality of diction. . . . The threat has nothing of passion in it." "Every aspect of the play—structure, characterization, style . . . celebrates the victory of form over disorder and chaos."

This is surely inadequate. Because propagandists and ad-men assert, "What I say three times is true," must we remain forever in the limbo of pre-stressed formalist anesthesia? Shakespeare understood the demon better than that.

36. Harry Levin, "The Shakespearean Overplot," *Renaissance Drama*, VIII, 1965, 63–71; 71.

37. A. P. Rossiter (*Angel With Horns*, pp. 254-55), for all his grasp of Shakespeare's *change* from traditional formulations, makes much of his casual and apparently conventional use of the words "tragedy" and "tragic(al)." He notes, without pursuing inferences, that the only time the words are used with "philosophical implications" is in *Titus Andronicus:* "Oh, why should nature build so foul a den, / Unless the gods delight in tragedies?" (IV.i.59-60) I find this significant: thus early, Shakespeare had penetrated to the heart of the matter with a preview-question of Lear's "Is there any cause in nature that makes these hard hearts?" He had emphasized the exigence of it in the previous scene of *Titus Andronicus;* the messenger bringing Titus his sons' heads and his own cut-off hand, philosophizes on the ways of (god-like) Emperors: "Thy griefs their sports, thy resolution mocked;" and Marcus Andronicus picks it up: "These miseries are more than to be borne. To weep with them that weep doth ease some deal, But sorrow flouted at is double death." (III.1.238; 244-46)

38. In *A Midsummer Night's Dream*, an early and "comedy-oriented" inquiry into the capacity of godlike reason and power to make something of constancy out of the tangled chains of imagination and the customary crosses of love, Theseus and Oberon and their consorts stand for the gods. Theseus's regal attempt to make silk purses out of sow's ears ("The worst are no worse if imagination amend them") is rendered dubious by Hippolyta's realization that "It must be *your* imagination, then, and not theirs." Earlier in the same scene Theseus has declared it the intent and desire of "noble respect" to pick a welcome out of silence, but this movement in the direction of kindness (and Hippolyta's in the direction of pity) undergoes near fatal vicissitudes as the godlike observers of the players try to find the concord of their discord: the would-be noble beasts, man and lion, turn in their mouths into foxes, geese, cats, and asses. And we have seen earlier, too, that Theseus's divine prerogative of making honors out of impossibilities, *aliquid ex nihilo*, is really exercised for his own delectation: Philostrate, the Duke's master of revels, says the play "is nothing, nothing in the world— Unless *you* can find *sport* in their intents." Theseus acknowledges the ultimate primacy of *his* gratification: "The kinder we, to give them thanks for nothing. Our *sport* shall be to *take* what they mistake." Theseus's brusque dismissal of the troupe at the end renders highly unlikely their being "made men"; there is no sign of Bottom's getting his sixpence for life. And this had been prefigured when Oberon, trying to make amends for the bad side effects of his own willful reassertion of

lordship over Titania, tells Puck (*his* master of illusions) to provide a remedy. Puck raises the same question as Philostrate: "Shall we their fond pageant see? Lord, what fools these mortals be!" Oberon at least tacitly agrees ("Stand aside") with Puck's assessment of the result: "Then will two at once woo one, That must needs be *sport* alone." All this, of course, had been tried out earlier yet, in *Love's Labour's Lost.* The Princess-goddess ("Nor God, nor I, delight in prejured men"), intending to cross the intents of her mighty opposites, anticipates Hamlet's deriving sport from hoisting the enginer with his own petar— "There's no such sport as sport by sport o'er thrown"—and, in overruling the King's refusal to salvage something from his debacle by presenting a "show worse than the King's and his company," is even more direct than Theseus in exploiting the good bowlers in the same way:

> That sport best pleases that doth least know how,
> Where zeal strives to content, and the contents
> Dies in the zeal of that which it presents.
> Their form confounded makes most form in mirth
> When great things laboring perish in their birth. ·

Mercade, the ambassador of death, is welcomed, except that he interrupts the merriment of the noble respecters, who have been engaged in retrieving some of their loss of face by putting the o'erparted players out of countenance. It is not generous, not gentle, not humble; gods, or men who would be like gods, find such virtues incompatible with their natures, or their honors, or their sport.

39. Compare the Lord of the Hebrew patriarchs and prophets and kings:

> And I, behold, I will harden the hearts of the Egyptians, and they shall follow them: and I will *get me honor* upon Pharoah. . . . And the Egyptians shall know that I am the Lord, when I have *gotten me honor* upon Pharoah. (*Exodus*, 14:17-18)

> . . . ye shall be a *peculiar* treasure *unto me* above all people: for the earth is *mine.* (*Exodus*, 19:5)

> . . . the LORD thy God hath chosen thee to be a special people *unto himself.* (*Deuteronomy*, 7:6)

> For the Lord will not forsake his people *for his great name's sake.* (1 *Samuel* 12:22)

The Lord God hath sworn *by himself*, saith the LORD God of hosts,
I abhor the excellency of Jacob. (*Amos*, 6:8)

(King James Version; emphasis added.)
    40. Harry Levin, *The Question of Hamlet*, New York, Oxford Univ.
Press, 1959, pp. 158–59.
    41. John D. Rosenberg, in "King Lear and his Comforters" (*EIC*,
XVI, April 1966, 135–46), has done half the job of writing this devoutly
to be wished for "epitaph on the last half-century of criticism upon
King Lear." But even he exempts Cordelia from the general curse, takes
the "Let's away to prison" speech at face value, and, reading "the clearest gods, who make them honours of men's impossibilities" as praise,
explains the uneasiness he feels in connection with the lines as a failure
of Shakespeare "to realize his intention *dramatically*." He asserts (and
demonstrates) that "we must learn once again to read the play as the
tragedy of King Lear, not his redemption, keeping this hard fact in the
centre of the stage of our minds, as Shakespeare always does." Indeed,
we must; and it is the hard words which help us to do so.
    William R. Elton in his massive demonstration against the Christian-
izers (*King Lear and the Gods*, San Marino, Huntington Library, 1966)
also fails (or perhaps declines as unnecessary?) to go beyond his find-
ings for sequential irony as the play's structure into the evidence that
even the *prisca theologia* of the good pagans—Cordelia, Edgar, Kent—
is subject to scrutiny and critique. Misgivings about the disinterestedness
and selflessness of these characters' virtue *do* arise, and are given shrewd
voice even in the very teeth of their most appealing heroics: Cornwall
(in Elton's scheme, one of "the fierce wrathful, [who] know nothing of
the light"—p. 293) does not merely blast Kent with unthinking retalia-
tory fury, but anatomizes the defects of his virtue in its genuine aspects
as well:

> These kind of knaves I know, which in their plainness
> Harbor more craft and more corrupter ends
> Than twenty silly ducking observants
> That stretch their duties nicely.   (II.ii.107–10)

Elton (p. 294) cites only the immediately preceding lines descriptive of
Kent himself, and concludes that "Although . . . he parallels Kent, Cornwall ironically indicts him as hypocritical." I assume this to mean a fairly
low-level dramatic irony, directed at Cornwall himself. But the contin-
uation of the speech is of a kind with the other "indictments" in the play

—against "the superfluous and lust-dieted man" or "that nature which contemns it origin" or "yond simpering dame . . . that minces virtue" or the Justice who "rails upon yond simple thief."

When we enter the domain of irony as structure, it is difficult to know where it stops; at least, Shakespeare does not provide us with unequivocal boundary lines.

42. *Measure for Measure*, for example, hangs perilously on "good" trickery: the Duke-Friar tells Isabella that what he suggests is all right, since "the doubleness of the benefit defends the deceit from reproof," and tells Mariana that " 'tis no sin, Sith that the justice of your title to him Doth flourish the deceit." This, with the insistent coupling of *strangeness* and *abuse* with *truth*, and the playing-around with the various meanings and modes of "knowing," in the last scene-act, shows Shakespeare to be under the thrall of the tricksy demon. Isabella, after pointing out that the Duke's original reference of her to Angelo for justice is bidding her to "seek redemption of the Devil," uses part of Helena's language and rhetoric in her plea for boldness: "I conjure thee, as thou believest There is another comfort than this world. . . . Make not impossible That which but seems unlike. . . . but let your reason serve To make the truth appear where it seems hid, And hide the false seems true." Leviathan can be drawn out only by hook or crook.

David L. Stevenson (*The Achievement of Shakespeare's Measure for Measure*, Ithaca, Cornell Univ. Press, 1966) makes a persuasive case for the play as "designed to release or unlock our inner world of sexual 'knowing' and our inner world of noninstitutionalized moral cognition and judgment" (p. 5). He emphasizes the "haunting moral ambiguities we find lurking below the surface of our own behavior—and enriching it" (p. 62). "All attempts to make *Measure for Measure* into an analogue of religious doctrine, or some kind of religious allegory or parable, heavily restrict and *contain* its inferential power" (p. 111; emphasis added). Stevenson does good work against the theologizers, but perhaps throws the baby out with the bath; and, from my point of view, unnecessarily obscures his very considerable penetration into the thing contained in this dramatic poem by retreating into the twin parameters of dramatic structure and moral humanism, as his substitutes for "gross religious assertions."

43. Kafka, *The Great Wall of China*. Cited from J. Hillis Miller, "Franz Kafka and the Metaphysics of Alienation," in Scott, op. cit., pp. 282, 293, 298.

44. There is, of course, the usual amount of general *reference* to "the

gods," "ye gods"; but this kind of thoughtless mild expletive is rarely in Shakespeare more than an automatic rubbing of a good-luck charm. Scarus, in a passion, reduces the gods to a ludicrous caboodle of ineffectual superstitions: "Gods and goddesses, All the whole synod of them!" Even a momentary upgrading of it to a formal exchange of official pieties (as we have seen, see note 87 to ch. 1) immediately gives way to a Roman self-sufficiency. Thomas MacFarland has established the worldliness of the Roman values in the play (op. cit, pp. 92–110).

45. In the very scene in which Antony is certified as Lord of Lords (and Cleopatra as "this great fairy") he commends his Macbeth-like warrior Scarus to Cleopatra's blessing and favoring hand, inasmuch as "He hath fought today As if a god in hate of mankind had Destroyed in such a shape." Immediately preceding, Antony has promised Scarus reward "Once for thy spritely comfort, and tenfold For thy good valor"; this, in response to Scarus's "Let us score their backs, And snatch 'em up, as we take hares, behind. 'Tis *sport* to maul a runner."

46. Cleopatra, when she feels immortal longings, determines to assuage them by being noble to herself. The worm and the vile world (see Murray Krieger's discussion of this seemingly obsessive trope in the Sonnets, in *A Window to Criticism*) are left to Caesar; and Cleopatra hears Antony "mock the luck of Caesar, which the gods give men to excuse their after wrath." And Charmian is given our phrase, identifying the gods themselves with (Cleopatra's) *modus vivendi et operandi,* dissolution:

Dissolve, thick cloud, and rain, that I may say
The gods themselves do weep!

47. Samuel Johnson, notes to *Cymbeline,* ed. 1765; cited from *Samuel Johnson on Shakespeare* (ed. W. K. Wimsatt, Jr.), New York, Hill and Wang, 1960, p. 108.

Interpretation of Shakespeare (notably, at present, of the Final Plays) from a depth-psychology orientation corroborates, I believe, at least part of the foregoing analysis.

48. *Reaper* is a complex word in Shakespeare. See, for example, *Coriolanus* I.iii.35 ff. (Volumnia envisages her son plucking Aufidius down by the hair):

His bloody brow
With his mailed hand then wiping, forth he goes,
Like to a harvestman that's tasked to mow
Or all, or lose his hire.

1. Miguel de Unamuno, *The Tragic Sense of Life in Men and Peoples* (trans. J. E. Crawford Flitch), London, Macmillan, 1921; Arnold, "The Scholar Gypsy", 1853, "Stanzas From The Grande Chartreuse," 1855; Morton D. Zabel, ed., *The Portable Conrad*, New York, Viking, 1949, p. 4; W. J. Cash, *The Mind of the South*, New York, Knopf, 1941, p. 74.

2. Adams, *Strains of Discord*, pp. 50, 69, 136, 162, 210–11.

3. Barbara Hardy, in *The Appropriate Form, An Essay on the Novel* (London, Athlone, 1964), argues for tension between the aesthetic form and what she calls "truthfulness." Her position may be subject to Douglas Hewitt's strictures on the score of theory of the novel (review, *EIC*, XVI, 1966), but I find it very persuasive in terms of our classic form of tragedy.

4. Cited from *The Portable Conrad*.

5. Conrad, cited from *The Portable Conrad*, pp. 712–13.

6. Conrad, *Author's Note;* cited from *Lord Jim*, ed. Moser, p. 1. (See n. 20 below)

7. Morton D. Zabel, ed. *Lord Jim*, Boston, Houghton Mifflin, 1958, p. xxvi.

8. Adams, ch. VIII, pp. 180–200.

9. Lawrence is a fascinating source for many of the ideas in this study, but a dangerous tiger to tie oneself to. Certainly a radical romantic with a powerful sense of the demonic; insistent upon a self-determining form, and claiming that true knowledge resides in the unconscious, the "fourth dimension;" impatient with some of the more obvious "tragic" manifestations—

> Tragedy seems to me a loud voice
> Louder than is seemly.

> Tragedy looks to me like man
> In love with his own defeat.
> Which is only a sloppy way of being in love with yourself.

> I can't very much care about the woes and tragedies
> Of Lear and Macbeth and Hamlet and Timon.
> They cared so excessively themselves.

(CP 508; Gordon, p. 79)

—he nevertheless kept on shifting his own terms and constructing new symbolic systems to take the place of those he denounced as prisons of the dynamic daemon. He laid on his own containers, new coercive, non-aesthetic roles for his vital being to play—a "nemesis to an evil civilization," for example (Gordon, p. 90). He accepts hastily the Hegelian and sociological notion of tragedy, and puts one of his seminal ideas to work on this straw man, trying to demonstrate, as Gordon says (p. 75), "that a more life-enhancing, visionary significance, present in latent form in the work but unconscious in the artist, could be rescued from the intended and manifest tragic meaning." "After 1925 Lawrence's sense of promise, like his health, becomes noticeably more frail. Demonism attenuates into satire" (p. 91). Yes: and his radical romanticism, unlike Conrad's, could never quite utter itself in the true voice of tragedy.

10. Conrad, cited from *The Portable Conrad*, p. 706, p. 712; Conrad, *A Personal Record*, cited from *Joseph Conrad on Fiction* (ed. W. F. Wright), Lincoln, Univ. of Nebraska Press, 1964, p. 147; letter to Madame Poradowska, August 26, 1891.

11. Kenneth Muir, *Last Periods of Shakespeare, Racine, Ibsen*, Detroit, Wayne State Univ. Press, 1961, p. 56.

12. The obsessive use of the phrase throughout Marlow's various narrative modes (nine times, by my count), and Conrad's putting it in inverted commas as the last word of the Author's Note, raises speculation as to how strongly—and consciously—Conrad thought of himself as at least analagous to the agonized Creator in *Genesis*, Who having made man in His own image and likeness found that man was indeed "become as one of us, to know good and evil." In nearly every instance in *Lord Jim* the context of the phrase has some intimation that Jim was Adamic: "He stood there for all the parentage of his kind" (27); "some conviction of innate blamelessness" (48–49); "as though he had been an individual in the forefront of his kind . . . mankind's conception of itself" (57); "he was too much like one of us not to be dangerous" (65); "He existed for me, and after all it is only through me that he exists for you" (137); "one could almost envy him his catastrophe" (197); "to the world he had renounced, and the way at times seemed to lead through the very heart of untouched wilderness" (201); "Jim's racial prestige and the reputation of invincible, supernatural power" (220); "have I not stood up once, like an evoked ghost, to answer for his eternal constancy?" (253). (Page numbers from Moser, op. cit.)

The satanic Gentleman Brown has his own version of this complicity, "a subtle reference to their common blood . . . a sickening suggestion of common guilt. . . ."

Was it the realization that he had evoked the demonic in man, in creating Jim, that finally forced Conrad to give him a tragic end—lest he (heroically romantic) take also of the tree of life, and eat, and live forever? Piety binds both ways; tragic man postulates a tragic God. The author of a tragic tale must undergo the sombre stress, *usque ad finem.*

13. Cited from *The Portable Conrad*, pp. 734-35.

14. Zabel, *The Portable Conrad*, p. 14.

15. Conrad, "A Familiar Preface," *Conrad's Prefaces to his Works* (ed. E. Garnett), London, Dent, 1937, p. 207.

16. Eliot, quoted in F. Scott Fitzgerald, *The Crack-Up* (ed. Edmund Wilson), New York, New Directions, 1931, p. 310. Fitzgerald, letter to H. L. Mencken (May or June, 1925). Cited from *The Letters of F. Scott Fitzgerald* (ed. Andrew Turnbull), New York, Scribners, 1963, p. 482.

17. Some corroboration of all this as a continuing preoccupation of the self-conscious Bloomsburian sensibility—which Conrad may be said to have anticipated, or even created—can be found in Virginia Woolf's *Orlando* (New York, Harcourt, Brace, 1928):

> It is all an illusion (which is nothing against it, for illusions are the most valuable and necessary of all things, and she who can create one is among the world's greatest benefactors), but it is notorious that illusions are shattered by conflict with reality, so no real happiness, no real wit, no real profundity are tolerated where the illusion prevails. (p. 181)

> A man who can destroy illusions is both beast and flood. Illusions are to the soul what atmosphere is to the earth. Roll up that tender air and the plant dies, the colour fades. The earth we walk on is a parched cinder. It is marl we tread and fiery cobbles scorch our feet. By the truth we are undone. Life is a dream. 'Tis waking that kills us. He who robs us of our dreams robs us of our life—(and so on for six pages if you will, but the style is tedious and may well be dropped.) (pp. 185-86)

But the self-mocking tone can't keep itself alive, and needs the Conradian cadences to feed on: very soon after we get

> "What's an 'age', indeed? What are 'we'?" and their progress through Berkeley Square seemed the groping of two blind ants, momentarily thrown together without interest or concern in common, across a blackened desert. She shivered. But here again was darkness. Her illusion revived. (p. 186)

[At midnight at the end of the eighteenth century] a huge blackness sprawled over the whole of London. The great cloud . . . hung, not only over London, but over the whole of the British Isles on the first day of the nineteenth century. . . . A change seemed to have come over the climate of England. . . . The sun shone, of course, but . . . its beams were discoloured and purples, oranges, and reds of a dull sort took the place of the more positive landscapes of the eighteenth century. (pp. 204–205)

These locutions and phrasings and images owe themselves, perhaps, to the Conrad-Marlow of *Heart of Darkness*—even though Orlando's earlier experience of confusion and obscurity had been shared by Mr. Pope of the *Dunciad*.

18. Zabel, *The Portable Conrad*, p. 19.

19. Conrad, Preface to *The Nigger of the Narcissus*, cited from *The Portable Conrad*, p. 708.

20. Data for a chronology of the conception, writing, revision, and publication of *Lord Jim* are presented in a most helpful form in pages 275–306 of the Norton Critical Edition, edited by Thomas C. Moser (New York, 1968). Most of the critics who have dealt with "how *Lord Jim* came into being" (p. 276)—including Conrad himself, in his letters and prefaces—seem to find the significant break, the unpremeditated development, to come at the end of the *Patna* episode: for better or for worse, it came out as a two-part book. But the tale's sense of an ending changed and developed in spite of its author, and the data are sufficiently ambiguous, I believe, to be susceptible of a different grouping. For example, on February 14, 1899 Conrad wrote to Blackwood: "I have a story *Jim* half-written or one-third written (10,000 words) . . . there are with Youth (13,000) and H. of D. (38,000) say 50 to 52 thousand words ready. *Jim* being 20 or 30 thou. would almost make up matter enough for a book." By September 6 he could foresee that "the story will be fully 40,000 words," but was still planning to end it romantically: "The important thing now for me is to get rid of my deplorable Jim with honour and satisfaction to all concerned." On January 1, 1900 he wrote to Garnett: "You cannot possibly know where I tend and how I shall conclude this most inconclusive attempt . . . the surprise reserved for you will be in the nature of a chair withdrawn from under one; something like a bad joke . . . ." By February 2 he was more sanguine: "*it* comes! *it* comes!" and in April he could "assure" Blackwood "that *Lord Jim has* an end . . . and I am now trying to write it out."

I find that the qualitative and decisive change comes between the *Patna*-Patusan story and the Gentleman Brown story and that, far from being, as Conrad called it, a plague spot resulting from "the division of the book into two parts," it was a providential beauty spot earned by Conrad's loyalty to the inner necessity of his tragic vision of romance.

21. R. C. Stephens ("Heart of Darkness: Marlow's Spectral Moonshine," *EIC*, XIX, 3, July 1969, 273–84) provides a critique of the foregoing customary reading of the novella, questioning the sincerity of Marlow's declared motives and finding him an egotistical, self-deluded hungerer after a spurious "more metaphysical" dimension of the real horror of "unchecked imperialistic exploitation" (279; 275). "Posing as a Buddha preaching in European clothes, he sits mesmerized and helpless before his own phantoms, but he will never hold the lotus-flower of self-forgetfulness" (282). His irony is "grim and cynical" and incomprehensible if we try to take it at face value (284).

Stephens reads the story as an (unsuccessful) attempt by Conrad to purge himself of his own "guilt"; his conclusion implies that *we* should be inspired to rather more skepticism than the "faint uneasiness" that the author himself admits feeling about Marlow. As a direct appraisal of *Heart of Darkness* alone—or with referents outside the story only to Conrad's biography—this is difficult to quarrel with. But if the story is indeed part of a continuing development of the Marlow-persona, the author-as-tragic-hero surrogate, I find it more helpful to accept and absorb the data as the story-teller gives them; Conrad is trying, above all, to make me *see*, and is perhaps more aware than most tragic writers of the danger of too much ironic containment. He is by no means done with Marlow, that seeker after the knowledge of good and evil.

22. Flying touches of reminiscence to Shakespearean characters (doubtless unconscious—Conrad knew Shakespeare well; his father had translated him into Polish) flash out to the reader who is ready for them: Brown is a demidevil Iago, with the "satanic gift of finding out the best and the weakest spot in his victims," and Jewel, like Desdemona no moth of peace, "showed an extraordinary martial ardor." There is an eerie parallel between Stephano with Caliban, and Brown with Cornelius—this last a monstrous deformity who takes to bolting out, "vermin-like, from the long grass growing in a depression of the ground" and who later is "mute as a fish," alleging that Jim, whom he also knew well, had come to Patusan and robbed him of his plunder and insisting that Brown "kill him the first chance you get, and then you can do what you like." Brown is seen "working himself into a fury of hate and

rage against those people who dared defend themselves"; "What's that to me that they are unoffending when I am starving for next to no offense?" It may be over-subtle, but I cannot help remembering Henry V at Harfleur, telling *those* besieged citizens that they were guilty in defense: "What is it then to me if impious war. . . ." When Brown delivers his "act of cold-blooded ferocity" as he escapes, he does it as an *acte gratuit* to "balance his account with the evil fortune." Marlow worries it:

> Notice that even in this awful outbreaking there is a superiority as of a man who carries a right—the abstract thing—within the envelope of his common desires. It was not a vulgar and treacherous massacre; it was a lesson, a retribution; a demonstration of some obscure and awful attributes of our nature which, I am afraid, is not so very far under the surface as we like to think.

(Think of Brutus; Henry V.; Othello; the justice of it pleases.) Jim, we recall, had exulted "It was immense!" at his victorious massacre at the stockade, where his chosen henchman, Macbeth-like Tamb' Itam, had "distinguished himself by the methodical ferocity of his fighting."

4. FAULKNER: SAYING NO TO DEATH

1. Review of *The Faulkner Reader*, N. Y. *Times* Book Review, April 4, 1954, p. 1. Howe characterizes Faulkner's foreword to the volume, which includes the phrase "say No to death," as "undistinguished and rather frenetic," and finds the true Faulknerian affirmation in the despair of *The Sound and the Fury* and the pastoralism of *The Bear* rather than in "the self-indulgent rhetoric of his recent speeches." One corroboration of this rather generally-held view appears in A. E. Hotchner's *Papa Hemingway* (New York, Random House, 1966); Hemingway retorted to reports of Faulkner's remarks on *Across the River and Into the Trees* (spring of 1951) with:

> Did you read his last book [? *Requiem for a Nun*]? It's all sauce-writing now, but he was good once. Before the sauce, or when he knew how to handle it. You ever read his story "The Bear"? Read that and you'll know how good he once was. But now . . . well, for a guy who runs as a silent, he sure talks a hell of a lot.

2. *The Pilgrim's Regress*. See my earlier attempt to draw upon this insight in "The Possibility of a Christian Tragedy," note 23 for ch. 1.

3. Faulkner, *Paris Review* interview; cited from *Bear, Man, and*

God (hereafter referred to as *BMG*) (ed. Utley, Bloom, and Kinney), New York, Random House, 1964, p. 124.

4. Hemingway (Hotchner, op. cit. pp. 69–70) and many other well-qualified critics, with whom I agree about Faulkner's abuses, as one does with F. R. Leavis about Conrad's. But there can be no entry into the lists of literary majority without depositing some forfeit; and Hemingway's own "older and simpler and better words" and rhetoric are subject to a comparable charge of pretentiousness and the dry mock of parody. Ben Jonson was as censorious about Spenser and Donne and Daniel—and his judgments have proved to be less than definitive.

5. Adams, pp. 190–92.

6. *The New Yorker*, XXXV, 29, Sept. 5, 1959, 103–04.

7. Gene Bluestein ("The Blues as a Literary Theme," *Massachusetts Review*, VIII, 4, 1967, 593–617), while not crediting Faulkner with complete or satisfactory rapport with the "meaning or function of blues in Negro tradition," finds him "incredibly accurate in his description of what the music sounded like" (599); and he quotes Ralph Ellison on the "desire to express an affirmative way of life. . . . Life could be harsh, loud, and wrong if it wished, but they [the jazzmen] lived it fully, and when they expressed their attitude toward the world it was with a fluid style that reduced the chaos of living to form." (612–13)

8. A few attempts have been made, notably among the Christian apologists, to rebaptize the tragic Thing. Nelvin Vos's *The Drama of Comedy: Victim and Victor* (Richmond, John Knox Press, 1966) tries to have all the death-forces swallowed up in his Christian-dramatic-Dantean rubric; he recruits Ionesco, for example, with statements such as "It is evident that Ionesco employs comic structure in his drama for the simple reason that the comic is the most powerful medium to convey the desperate and tragic absurdity of man's existence." I do not find this kind of ideological collapsing of the spectrum more convincing than the technical spreading of it to accommodate another genre (see note 12 to ch. 1 on Guthke's *Tragicomedy*) and hope to avoid it in the present discussion.

9. The temptation is strong, in dealing with Faulkner as with any writer of an essentially mythic imagination, to find analogues with the great epic and tragic stories of the past; nor, I think, is it improper to yield to it if one can keep it under control. This Aeneas comparison is just the kind of thing Faulkner himself tosses in; and he has spoken of his own various cycles of stories as sagas. As late as *The Rievers*, he gives the patriarch of the whole inbred clan, Lucius Quintus Carrothers,

the status of universality through initials—LQC (like Joyce's HCE?),
a kind of post-Roman aristocratic Everyman—and casually labels him
"time-honored Lancaster." He alludes to Flem Snopes as an established
mythical personage: "when Mr. Flem Snopes (the banker murdered ten
or twelve years ago by the mad kinsman who perhaps didn't believe his
cousin had actually sent him to the penitentiary but at least could have
kept him out or anyway tried to) began to lead his tribe out of the
wilderness behind Frenchman's Bend, into town . . . ."

10. H. M. Campbell and R. E. Foster (*William Faulkner: A Critical
Appraisal*, Norman, Univ. of Oklahoma Press, 1951) point out "the
atmospheric function of Faulkner's humor, the use of humor to give an
emotional ambivalence to a scene—the guarded style," and show the
possibility of a "delayed reaction" whereby "the horror may be in-
creased by the very casualness of the humorous contrast offered" (p.
111); they speak of Faulkner's imagery as useful "finally . . . for embody-
ing the very bitter satire which seems inspired by his comprehensive
pessimistic philosophy" (p. 40). I would enlist these very perceptive
remarks for our putative tragic Faulkner, rather than a bitterly satiric
one.

11. I do not want to elevate unduly my troll-under-the-bridge trope
(though indeed the folktale is an archetype), but backing for it can be
found plentifully in Faulkner, who uses the bridge-ford-crossing situation as a central ordeal in many of his tragic or comitragic stories. This
time the protean troll has taken on the shape of one of the pony-rabbit-
parrot-deer-dove-squirrel-rattlesnake-pinwheel monsters, and, having
been fetched back from exile (in Texas), takes the bridge and its guard-
ian-users by surprise and storm; there is no Billygoat Gruff on duty, and
the troll goes *over* the bridge, blocking and shattering it enroute; nor
does he subside again underneath, but inhabits and possesses the upper
world, soaring, expanding, fiendish—out of the bottle for good: "Far
up the road now, distancing the frantic mules, the pony faded on."

12. Campbell and Foster, p. 136.

13. R. W. B. Lewis makes a persuasive case, on grounds of structure,
chronology-memory, and style, for Faulkner's strategy of containment:
"it is quite exact to say that the whole of the fourth section [the colloquy in the commissary between McCaslin Edmonds and Ike] is contained within the sections which have the wilderness as their setting"
(p. 315). However, Lewis has already decided that the strategy *works:*
"The action in Section Four is made possible by the experience preced-

ing it: the ritual in the wilderness *contains* the decision in the commissary" (p. 314). Indeed, he begins his essay with the postulate that *The Bear* is pivotal in Faulkner because there, for the first time, "what is positive in human nature and in the moral structure of the world envelops and surrounds what is evil; which is to say, more significantly, that the corrupting and the destructive and the desperate in human experience become known to us in their opposition and even their subordination to the creative and the soul-preserving" (p. 307). It is only when one brings the analytic activity of the critical demon within Faulkner himself to bear on this hopeful view that it is seen as a valiant but ultimately abortive attempt at "the transmutation of power into charity" (p. 322).

(The page references in parentheses above are to the reprint of Lewis's article in *BMG*. This compilation of "Seven Approaches to . . . *The Bear*" is an excellent repository of materials relevant to our subject, and I use it gratefully as a reference and quotation source.)

14. The *Ode on a Grecian Urn* is perhaps the high-water mark of the achievement by romanticism of a piercing tragic insight tamed by form: the resolution, the all-sufficient equation, Beauty is Truth, Truth Beauty: That is all you know on earth, and all you need to know. It is formulaic, like the similar (but obverse, negative) equalities enounced by the tragic oracle: ripeness is all; the readiness is all; all is vanity.

15. Here is the insistent little qualifier again. It fits into Faulkner's total rhetorical strategy as a variant of the fourth item ("a negative or a series of negatives followed by a positive") of W. V. O'Connor's list of rhetorical devices (*BMG*, p. 344). Somewhat as philosophies of *as if* try to provide escape hatches, it fights the demon of negation by putting a floor, a *terminus a quo*, one end of a container, under the plunge toward nihilism.

16. R. W. B. Lewis, "The Hero in the New World: William Faulkner's *The Bear*," BMG, pp. 308–309.

17. Hemingway, in an analytical moment, is illuminatingly candid: "I'll tell you, even though I am not a believer in analysis, I spend a hell of a lot of time killing animals and fish so I won't kill myself. When a man is in rebellion against death, as I am in rebellion against death, he gets pleasure out of taking to himself one of the godlike attributes, that of giving it" (Hotchner, p. 139).

18. See especially D. H. Stewart, H. A. Perluck, and (partly) W. F. Taylor, in *BMG*.

19. Interview, cited from Arthur F. Kinney, " 'Delta Autumn': Post-lude to *The Bear*," *BMG*, p. 393.

20. The timing remains inferential; however, the *Saturday Evening Post* version of *The Bear* came out on May 9, 1942; in the *Go Down Moses* version (published in 1942) *Delta Autumn* immediately follows *The Bear*. Arthur F. Kinney (*BMG*, 384–95) calls *Delta Autumn* a "Postlude to *The Bear*." His essay offers many perceptive and telling readings of it as "Ike's failure," but at the end returns to the salvationist camp: "For Ike has only apparently failed . . . . The moment of horror is also the moment of hope . . . the crime is also its own solution . . . the man who has fallen is yet free to act." I do not find any literary evidence in the story of these transformations.

21. This change in the character of the overplot, from the earlier notion of Nature's *cyclical* but ever life-renewing metamorphosis to a *linear*, one-way degenerative mutability, is powerful evidence of Faulkner's being in tune with the deeply tragic, that which we have glimpsed in the physicists' intimations of entropy and in Conrad's and Stevenson's intimations of annihilation. Where before he had been able to work within the redemptive time scheme of succeeding generations contained within a self-regenerative wilderness-land (putting off the vision of a "worthless tideless rock cooling in the last crimson evening" with an *until* clause), now the failure to transfer values between generations is pre-figured in the necessity of the hunters to follow the retreating wilderness to the verge of its enemy ocean, practically to land's end. Where before the wilderness was circumscribed (Sutpen's Hundred, for example: a block of land ten miles square), now it is laid open to irretrievable engulfment: the Delta is an open-ended triangle. They can reach the small apex of wilderness-land only by water; and it is slipping down into the sea as they tramp in it.

22. As maybe Hemingway was right: "The oldest double *dicho* I know," he told Hotchner (p. 73; 1953), "is: Man can be destroyed but not defeated." Like all such double sayings, it can have its inversion, and the possibility that the inversion is closer to the truth is what haunts the heart and the imagination of tragic writers. What keeps them going is the dialectic behind their own dual response: (1) "I've always perferred to believe that man is undefeated," said Hemingway; and the *dicho* itself was at the heart of *The Old Man and the Sea*, a salvationist work. (2) Hemingway summed up his feelings about death as "just another whore"; he had earlier hailed it as the virgin: "Hail nothing

full of nothing, nothing is with thee." He ridiculed "serious symbol-oriented, death-wish-oriented questions," but kept making "sublimations" anyway.

Hemingway and Faulkner complement and illuminate one another, and nowhere more than on this all-absorbing subject. Each had his own way, however, of being conversant with death, in literature and in life: and both, after saying Yes, and Maybe, and No in all the ways they could think of, finally acquiesced in the death-wish-fulfillment.